THE CODER'S
LEGAL GUIDE

Mac O'Neill, Esq.

ISBN: 9781092468077

He who loves practice without theory is like the sailor who boards ship without a rudder and compass and never knows where he may cast.

— Leonardo da Vinci

CONTENTS

INTRODUCTION

Welcome and thank you for purchasing The Coder's Legal Guide. 2018 marks the 10th anniversary of both the Apple App Store and the Google Play store. Since Apple introduced the App Store on July 10, 2008, apps have changed the world in ways that were unimaginable perhaps even to Steve Jobs.

Apps have created a unique and powerful market with enormous opportunities for indie software developers. The objective of this book is to give coders a basic understanding of the legal issues presented by such a quickly evolving industry. Included are strategies that strengthen, add value to and protect a coder's products.

I hope you enjoy the book and find it useful.

DISCLOSURE & NOTICE

The contents of this book are intended solely for educational and informational purposes. The author is a former lawyer but does not currently hold an active professional license. No professional, attorney-client, lawyer-client or consultant-client relationship is intended between the author and reader in the sale, reading or use of this book.

The author is not responsible for any actions, errors, omissions or liability resulting from the reader's use of or reliance on any information contained herein.

No part of this book may be reproduced or distributed without prior written consent.

ABOUT THE AUTHOR

The author is a former lawyer, software and business consultant that has worked with both large and small developers, publishers, international entertainment and media firms and startups for nearly 20 years.

He has extensive experience with intellectual property, risk assessment and avoidance and commercial agreements. His expertise ranges from one-person startups to international firms dealing with top tier entertainment and media brands.

He now writes on software, intellectual property, startup and media topics.

FOREWORD

Software development is an incredibly misunderstood process that portrays coders as recluses wielding almost wizard like power. In a room lit only by the soft glow of laptop clad in a skin of nerd culture stickers, the coder sits ultra-focused, filling the room with the cacophony of keystrokes and brutally anatomically correct expletives. Code flows from the fingertips, flawless in design, filing the screen like the mysteries of ancient runes. The next Candy Crush millionaire has created their opus.

The reality, however, is much more solemn. It begins with an idea, a flash of inspiration. Its lifeless form lingers in the creative mind, poked and prodded by relaxed but curious interest, until some motivating force propels it forward on its long journey toward life. A wayward conversation may fuel the subconscious with the raw materials needed to finish the dream. Everyday living might petulantly demand an evolutionary step toward something newer and greater than what came before. Or perhaps a revolution unfolds, devouring tired business models in its inescapable gravitational pull. Whatever the impetus, coders create not by choice but because they must.

Ideas unfold.

Code is written.

Apps are born.

The modern version of this process retains the traditional drive to create while differing radically in its practical application. In its former manifestation, the software marketplace was made up of vast, unending rows of cardboard boxes that arrived weekly and thereafter gathered dust. The luckier ones managed to capture the interest of a customer, who paid $50 and upwards for games and tools that were either passionately enjoyed or haphazardly tossed into a closet alongside a 10 year old Taekwando trophy.

Today, however, software is consumed instantly upon release, disks are ancient relics and the Internet makes it possible to heap mountains of praise on great applications while briskly ushering the less fortunate to a dark, foreboding thud in the cavernous digital underworld in a matter of minutes. Indeed, it was the Internet that quickly and powerfully transformed the software marketplace from its humble retail beginnings into the age of instant downloads, free trials, free-to-play and instant, automatic updates.

Yet, however irrevocably changed the delivery system may be, the software game remains largely the same. Apps still succeed or fail but they do so with breakneck speed. Popular apps skyrocket to stardom while those less fortunate are propelled equally as swiftly to a decidedly different fate. The challenge of persuading a user to fork over their hard-earned cash for software remains the same, but the transaction method has radically evolved.

Such a transformation has had profound effects on the software economy. Moreover, legal doctrines such as intellectual property and contract have been forced to rapidly evolve and change in response. Law has clumsily embraced the distribution of software in the App Era with an ongoing series of adaptations and sometimes bewildering rationalizations. As a result, the law as applied to software is currently a mishmash of old and new legal theory, a bug ridden alpha release that cannot maintain pace with technology. A particularly good example is the patent system, which is in serious disrepair. Under its auspices and using the vagaries of the system, lawsuits are used as a profitable business model by unscrupulous "troll" companies that create nothing, yet own a purportedly valuable patent.

Within this broken machine, an indie coder or small developer is ten times as likely to win a starring role in a multi-million dollar lawsuit as they are to produce a runaway best-selling app. On the flip side, if an outrageously popular app does result, a lawsuit is all but guaranteed once the patent trolls smell money. This rather dystopian result is rooted in the radical transformation of the software industry over the last ten years. Somewhere between here and there, the rules of the game changed but no one got the memo.

The unfortunate result is that coding in the App Era is the equivalent to stumbling onto a battlefield without knowing about the war. The questions indie coders must ask themselves before setting out to cross that field is "Who am I fighting and how do I survive?" Unfortunately, without preparation and a willingness to adapt, developers usually wind up fighting themselves.

As an intellectual property and technology attorney, I spent the better part of a decade advising software developers on legal and business issues. In recent years, there has been a fundamental shift in the nature of how coders interface with the seemingly esoteric world of the law. The legal aspects of an app now dictate its success and therefore dictate the success of a developer more than ever before.

This is very well illustrated by trolls, for whom lawsuits are an extremely lucrative business model. Such companies produce nothing, yet routinely use the threat of a lawsuit to coerce indie coders into unfair and onerous licensing agreements. Alternatively, trolls resort to an absurd series of claims, based on broadly written and horribly vague patents to threaten and extort a developer into either a pre-litigation "settlement." They thus win their battles without ever firing a shot.

Intellectual property law, indeed much of the legal process as a whole, has been hijacked by empty yet powerful players infected with the sickness of greed. And, unfortunately, these Mafioso-like thugs, armed with seemingly infinite resources and monolithic patent portfolios, have indie coders squarely in their sights. If a developer is targeted by a troll, the battle is not entirely lost but the shit has most definitely hit the fan.

Surviving trolls and other legal threats in the App Era is possible, but coders must arm themselves with a new set tools. In fact, the development process itself must evolve to incorporate the law and legal concepts as "frameworks" fundamental to the app and the developer's business. The perspective of coding itself must expand to include the law as a necessary component of the app itself, regardless of the scope or size of the project. Indeed, the App Era has created conditions such that the law now shapes an app and sometimes completely defines it.

There are a number of books about software development that primarily deal with managing and running things in the "leanest" and most efficient manner. Likewise, there are countless technical manuals focusing on the specifics of programming. One would think there would be a guide for coders to explain the core legal and business issues involved with running a software based enterprise, a book that puts the law of code into a meaningful context. Unfortunately, such a book does not exist, at least one not filled with case law citations and confusing legal jargon.

This is perplexing because legal rights have become such a critical part of an app and can often be a deciding factor in its ultimate success. These days, most indie coders are left scratching their heads and asking questions like, "What the hell is intellectual property and how does it affect my app?" or "Can I deal with this stuff later when I have more money?" Answering those and similar questions is why this book exists—to provide insight into the complex universe of legal issues that shape modern apps.

THE APP ERA

THE RISE OF THE MACHINES

Mobile apps dominate (and the term is used here in its most powerful and immediate sense) modern software. The spirited little buggers are tapped and flicked on more than 3 billion active smartphone devices worldwide in a market expected to exceed $92 billion by the end of 2018. Apple's App Store, which contained just 500 apps after its launch in 2008, now offers more than 2.2 million. Google's Google Play contains more than 3 million.

Apple's iPhone business alone would be a Fortune 100 company based on revenues. To put this in perspective, Apple's iPhone revenue in 2017 was greater than the entirety of Amazon's business. In 2012, a mere 5 years after the introduction of the iPhone, Apple's smartphone business was larger than Microsoft's entire lineup combined, a fact that still leaves many of the industry's old guard gasping for breath, especially as Apple recently became the world's first trillion dollar company.

To a large degree, the tremendous success of mobile devices has been driven by the apps that live on them. As of this writing, mobile users have downloaded more than 205 billion apps across the Apple App Store and Google Play platforms. Take a moment to really think about that.

205 billion.

According to most projections, the number of app downloads by 2021 will be more than 350 billion. This is, in a word, staggering. In 10 years, a mere decade, the principal method of software distribution has been completely revolutionized, with a growth rate that shows no signs of slowing or even pausing for a brief respite from the frenzy.

Yet, smartphones, while wonderful devices in and of themselves, have become the de facto monarchs of a technological renaissance solely because of apps and, therefore, coders. For all the marketing hype and lofty advertising speak, the mobile landscape would look extremely different if developers had not joined the party. Apple itself tacitly acknowledges this by advertising the iPhone and iPad not by specifications, but by showcasing the number of apps available in its App Store and the amount of revenue paid out to developers which, incidentally, is a mind boggling $100+ billion.

Quite simply, developers and their apps have been, are and continue to be the driving force behind the success of Apple, Google and the entire smartphone and mobile device industry in the App Era. To put it even more succinctly, without coders, the mobile landscape would be a dysfunctional wasteland of janky handsets and clumsy tablets serving as glorified notepads and calendars. Consider that for just a moment. Without developers, neither the smart device market nor Apple, currently the world's largest company, would exist in their present form.

Without those millions of indie coders cranking out the apps, iOS and Android would be meaningless buzzwords in a 3-star hotel seminar on getting things done. Apple would still be the red-headed stepchild of the technology industry and Samsung would be churning out clock radios of dubious quality. In terms of practical effect on the word at large, society would look shockingly different. People would still fumble with email, fervently believe SMS is "the wave of the future" and call each other via ancient, overpriced carriers.

There would be no quick game play on the way to work, no enraptured gazing at the pale blue glow on transcontinental flights, no quick and easy way to find out what friends and family are doing. There would be be no social-anything for that matter. Without apps, where would Twitter be today? How about Facebook or Instagram? Without modern devices and services made possible by apps, the President of the United States would have to scream mindlessly at his subordinates rather than to the public at large. Aside from the obvious benefit of the last point, the world would not be the same.

Despite their contributions, developers largely live in the shadow of the overall mobile ecosystem. It is a very odd circumstance—the people who create the products that revolutionized the world have the least amount of business and legal support. They have the smallest financial resources and minuscule net worths compared to the platform providers they have helped to become financial juggernauts. Even more alarming, one-hundred percent of the business and financial interaction between a user and an app occurs at the app store level, solely benefitting the platform provider's reputation and enabling them to completely control and manage the customer relationship.

While Apple and Google reap massive profits and increased brand recognition, coders are attacked and stripped of their success by trolls and corporate extortionists. They start the game with the deck stacked against them without resources to legal strategies that Apple and Google can easily implement. Even worse, the very system intended to promote development of new technologies, artistic expression and revolutionary inventions legitimizes the process. This situation, seemingly tolerated as a regrettable but tolerable side effect of intellectual property law, is the greatest threat to developers in the history of software.

True, many platform providers must battle their own legal wars but consider that the resources available to Apple or Google to fight those battles were, in large part, created by indie coders. Except for larger corporate shops, most developers do not have sufficient financial resources to fund the development of their app, let alone the potentially crushing legal costs and expenses associated with properly setting up shop and later defending it. This shocking state of affairs has yet to be addressed by the platform providers and will most likely remain the status quo.

Platform providers are thus the ultimate middlemen, growing their brand, increasing their hardware sales and enjoying a steady stream of new apps that fuel the demand. Despite this, indie coders do not have the resources and market position necessary to fully realize an intellectual asset or withstand a multimillion dollar lawsuit. Instead, most developers shoulder one-hundred percent of the legal and business responsibility for their products, from usability and compatibility to updates, along with the costs of litigation and expenses arising lawsuits. In return, they receive a fraction of the app's profits while the industry they created grows ever stronger. This is the digital equivalent of a serfdom, minus the benefits of protection by the lord's army.

It is therefore the legal cost associated with doing business in the App Era that is the primary barrier to entry for the vast majority of developers. It has become commonplace to simply ignore legal issues and either "wing it" or sideline issues to be "fixed" later. However, the law differs from coding in that there is no debug mode—some things cannot be hacked. Coders need change how they view legal and business strategies and seem them not as an expense but an essential part of the development process. Software developers are very much in a war where, unfortunately, they are the foot soldiers.

ACCESS DENIED

Popular culture views software programmers as idiosyncratic math savants with near superhuman abilities and a penchant for caffeine. Moreover, current mythology depicts the work of these fantastical creatures separating investors from their money with unnerving efficiency. In reality, however, most new coders fund their projects from the weekly food and beer budget or a loan from a "successful" sibling. Most developers nervously jump from one business plan to another before settling on one that at least somewhat resembles something that will garner investment. Afterwards, if they are determined and motivated enough, they convince other to join the fray and a company is born.

"Bootstrapping" is how most indie developers will

use to describe their finances if they are unfunded by an investor or venture group. This process, which closely resembles the otherworldly Jungian vision of a snake eating itself, is the business equivalent of the typical university student's ramen noodle diet. There are few things as exhilarating as successfully commanding a fledgling developer and steering it to victory and greatness. Conversely, bootstrapping a stagnant or unsuccessful venture is one of life's most frustrating and supremely anticlimactic experiences. Ironically, the results are often dictated not by a developer's products or vision but by the simple problem of gaining access to an increasingly crowded market.

Before the mobile app market exploded, when dinosaurs roamed the Earth, software was mostly controlled by a relatively small number of large developers. It was difficult, if not impossible, to make a dent in certain market segments, such as the ancient art of desktop publishing, principally because of the larger players. The near monopoly power wielded by those companies is still with us, evidenced by the dogged persistence of ".doc" files. However, on July 10th, 2008, the ability of small software developers to compete with the big-boys was changed forever with Apple's release of the App Store in iPhone OS 2.0, which has since been renamed "iOS" and is currently at version 12. Suddenly, developers of all sizes could get their apps straight into users' hands without distribution, packaging, shipping or any of the historical expenses of the retail-box software market.

A year later, the App Store was flooded with all manner of apps, from games and word processors to, yes, fart simulators. For a while, it seemed that the App Store was the best thing since sliced bread and/or air conditioning and developers of all sizes the world over sang its praises as the software delivery platform heralding a new golden age. As revolutionary as it was, and still is, the App Store brought with it a new symptom of the same disease.

The initial problem of access was solved by giving every coder ridiculously easy access to the same common digital shelf, regardless of physical location, number of employees or position on the Fortune 500. This was a revolution in every sense of the word. In a manner of moments, every developer on Earth (and I suppose even their slightly paler brethren hovering above) could participate in a ready-made digital marketplace with preexisting and pre-qualified customers. The credit card wielding pool of buyers tallied up over 10-million App Store downloads in 3 days, even though only 50 apps were available at launch. That number grew exponentially, of course, and astronomical download and revenue figures flooded the news.

The strategy was brilliant and generated tremendous iPhone sales for Apple. Users loved the idea, to say the least, as they suddenly had access to good quality, inexpensive games, social tools and an assortment of goofy yet addictive apps that filled the dips and valleys of modern living. For developers, it was a dream come true, a huge pool of buyers with valid credit cards and a demonstrated willingness to buy software, seemingly of any kind and nature. The app tidal wave crested a few years later, however, and it became apparent that the system had a rather unique flaw. It worked so well that it ultimately resurrected the overcrowded software shelf.

When there were fewer than 100,000 apps available in Apple's App Store, developers could easily and effectively reach a huge pool of potential users with relatively little effort. In 2018, however, more than 2.2 million apps are available. With so many available, it is incredibly difficult for developers to draw attention to their apps and, in turn, generate recurring sales. Even very good, well written products are simply lost in the sheer vastness of the modern App Store. The market is now dominated by a small number of incredibly successful apps by established developers, making it nearly impossible for solo and indie coders to find an audience. This is the App Era's analog to the dusty retail shelf—endless rows of apps on display and very few ways to get noticed.

As dysfunctional as the current App Store situation is, it is far better than shrink-wrapped boxes, breakage and transportation costs of the retail days. Yet the current predicament for developers that have the resources to churn out perhaps an app a year face nightmarish competition with larger, more prolific and heavily advertised competition. While this is not a strictly legal issue inasmuch as the solution might be as simple as throwing money at advertising or the sultry, shimmering hotness of social media, the problem of access to the app stores' customers does have significant legal implications.

Whenever there is a concentration of wealth, resources and power in a small number of market positions, there is a corresponding drop in innovation. Absent a disruptive event, such as Apple's release of the iPhone to a stagnant mobile phone industry in 2007, wealth and ownership is increasingly concentrated in larger, dominant industry participants. A particularly relevant example of this can be seen in the ownership of intellectual property in general and, particularly, in ownership of particular technology, software, frameworks and so-called "standards essential" patents. Nowhere is this concentration of power and its propensity for harm more readily observed than with trolls and their affect on indie developers.

Owning vast collections of patents, trolls will vigorously sue anyone with a pulse (and even that seems to be less of a prerequisite lately). In other words, wherever there is money to be found, trolls are sure to spontaneously appear and start sniffing. A glance at the statistics for mobile apps and the growth pattern of the industry in general quickly illustrates why trolls are so fond of suing coders these days. In the hopes of capturing the next hot-ticket app, trolls grow their "zombie army" of licensees by wildly throwing darts at a constantly growing universe of indie developers with a seemingly endless array of frivolous claims.

For example, one of the most notorious trolls, Lodsys, once pursued coders concerning an update technology implemented by Apple and Google as part of the platform. Yes, indie developers were sent demand letters and pursued in court for something they did not create or even implement. Why? Because if a troll fires off a lawsuit against Apple or Google, they know it will be a long, arduous journey to a settlement or any kind of damages award, if any. But fire that same lawsuit to hundreds of indie developers and at least a certain percentage of them will likely settle and sign a license agreement. Maybe, just maybe, one of those will go on to achieve runway success in the market, guaranteeing a hefty and regular stream of licensing revenue for the troll.

Quite simply, it is extremely difficult for developers to function alongside such monolithic impediments to innovation. The concentration of intellectual property ownership creates a situation where an indie coder has an exponentially higher likelihood of being dragged into a lawsuit than his retail-based predecessors. This has an extreme chilling effect on innovation. Developers either leave the market altogether or languish in a sea of litigation and legal fees.

There is, however, an alternative. Savvy coders have adapted by using the system against itself. These companies flourish, discovering niche markets and faithful audiences. They play outside the sandbox of their own development process, so to speak, as they redefine the notion of what an app is and how it is developed, protected and marketed. This requires tacit acceptance that an app is more than just code. Apps now require an elixir of coding and legal planing to survive, just as old-school floppy disk based apps required near magical memory management. In the App Era, coders must be as equally methodical at maximizing legal and business strategies.

BREAD & BUTTER

Indie coders and developers often cringe when discussing legal issues because mere mention of "law" evokes the image of chucking huge stockpiles of cash into a raging bonfire. In reality, such imagery results from the relatively disproportionate effect of legal expenses on observable results. It is easy to see changes from programming language revisions once an app is compiled, but law is quite a different beast. More often than not, legal costs are felt immediately whereas the effects are not be realized until much later. Moreover, some of those expenses may not yield results until the occurrence of a specific event. For example, if legal strategies have been implemented to reduce risk and liability, the effect will not be fully realized until fully litigated.

Because of this, attorneys and developers have historically had a relationship best likened to a marriage of convenience. Coders simply code and, if they are successful, money appears. And lawyers are usually the first person called when money is at stake. For various reasons, most lawyers disdain working with coders, whose cat-like attention span and idiosyncratic attitudes must be carefully introduced to the slow, lumbering world of law and the accompanying suit and tie. Nonetheless, as the industry developed over time, developers suddenly found themselves with money, cars and other things which owners generally want to protect. In the end, coders had money and lawyers tend to like money.

While developers still perceive lawyers with a certain vestigial stodginess, there is at least a growing acceptance of the fact that legal concepts are important in the software industry. High-profile lawsuits such as the Apple-Samsung matter have encouraged most developers to at least think about intellectual property, what it is and how to protect it. And, justifiably, trolls have also prompted serious concern. Faced with ever growing reports of demand letters and lawsuits, coders are keenly aware that the law, for better or worse, is a definite part of their business. Most now embrace, at least in layman's terms, basic legal concepts, such as intellectual property and contracts, as part of the game.

The traditional development paradigm must continue to evolve to include legal structures and "frameworks" along with programming languages, libraries and APIs. Surprisingly, this does not necessarily have to involve additional money being spent. Rather, developers should budget from the onset for legal analysis and counsel relating to their products and business. After all, in the App Era, the success or failure of an app could turn on a legal, rather than technical, issue. This perceptive may be criticized as simplistic but, in the long term, indie developers must do something to maintain the same level of competition against larger market forces. And part of that "something" is understanding that legal dollars must be spent in the same way as technical dollars.

Once again, it is very important to point out that rights to vast libraries of technologies and even the standards on which those technologies are based are quickly becoming concentrated in the hands of a very small group of wealthy entities. Indie developers, no matter how small, can use the same legal and business strategies used by the companies amassing money, power and market position. For example, and as we will discuss later, if a developer knows and understands their product at technical, business *and* legal levels, there is little need to fear a lawsuit. At a minimum, the developer will have structured its operations such that it will be an unattractive target for trolls and others that would seek to come knocking on the door.

There is no magic pill that takes care of this process, however. It requires acknowledgment that the law is (not just could be) an influential market factor and effective tool in the development process. It also demands a well formulated legal and business strategy and acceptance of responsibility at an almost parental level. Resources must be thought of as being "allocated for" rather than being "thrown away on" legal concerns. It would be a strange set of parents that argued against a critical expense for their child with the expectation that it can simply be dealt with a later time.

Imagine, for a moment, that a developer has a budget of $75,000, of which $15,000 can potentially be spent on legal expenses incident to starting the company, basic contracts, intellectual property concerns, etc. Rather than spend the money on legal fees, the choice is made to pour the $15,000 into additional coding work so that the project can be finished ahead of schedule. After its release, the app is a runaway success in the App Store and nets the developer millions of dollars in a relatively short period of time. It certainly seems like a great scenario—the developer saved money, finished ahead of schedule and made out like a bandit.

Further imagine that because certain legal work was never done, the contracts the developer pulled from the internet did not properly acquire ownership of the materials provided by the subcontractors that made the jump in release time possible. In this instance, fueled by eloquently written news reports of the Cinderella story out of nowhere that just made millions, the subcontractors approach the developer and demand a cut of the action. After quickly dismissing the claims and issuing a refusal, the subcontractors hire a lawyer, obtain an injunction to stop sales of the app and file a lawsuit seeking damages equal to or greater than the developer's profit plus additional damages.

It may seem ridiculous but, with just a fraction of its initial resources allocated for legal expenses, the entire dispute could have easily been avoided.

Moreover, had the developer approached the project with the integrated mindset mentioned above, those legal expenses may well have been worth many times what was actually paid after a dispute arose. This is an excellent example of the value of an investment being unknown until a later time. Indeed, in many cases, the true value of focusing on legal strategy as part of the development process will be impossible to reduce to a fixed sum of money.

The above catastrophe is extremely likely to occur without proper planning. Fortunately, they are easily avoided by disconnecting from traditional notions of sequestered development. Once released, an app, along with all of its weaknesses and those of its creator, is inextricably fused with the legal and business situation of the moment. Trolls, opportunists or even a jaded employee or disgruntled co-founder will latch onto those faults like a hungry shark. With a simple shift in expense allocation, developers can establish a defensible, adaptable legal and business structure that is capable of withstanding such attacks. When the developer and its business survive and prosper, the actualization of fully integrated development is complete.

THE CODE OF LAW

Every industry has its unique set of legal issues. Unfortunately for developers, theirs is a business that pushes the law to its limits. Even so, software startups tend to be confronted by the same basic legal problems as most other enterprises, at least during formation. Yet most developers enter the game without a fundamental understanding of core business issues. These include abstract legal entities having the same rights as people and property that can be owned, transferred, licensed or sold despite being mere construct. And popular media has somewhat glorified the fractious founder and partnership relationships that can dominate a developer's legal life in the initial years. But there is one issue concerning law and legal issues with which develops are suddenly and most definitely aware—money.

Adding the word "law" or "legal" to anything usually increases the cost significantly. Add to that the lingering uncertainty of the typical lawyers answer of, "It depends," and it is easy to understand why most small companies, software developers perhaps more so, loathe dealing with legal matters or anyone of the legal persuasion. Most indie coders eschew the dry, overly analytical world of the law and lawyers. Bu it is only by becoming as familiar with such things that a developer can increase the value of their apps and company.

The difficulty for indie coders is getting beyond the idea of the law and lawyers as "cost centers" where perfectly good money is sent to die a slow, painful death. This is no easy task, especially since most lawyers dealing with the issues presented by software development usually demand stratospheric rates. Compounding the analysis is the fact that some of he services they provide do not yield immediate results. Nonetheless, the law and its application may sometimes entirely determine the bundle of rights in a developer's app and its ultimate value. How the law does that is not directly observable and it is certainly not very straightforward.

Software development is demanding, requiring both technical skill and creative aspirations. The best applications implement and represent a developer's unique style. The practical aspect of coding an app involves countless hours of writing, debugging and rewriting code. Afterwards, even more time is spent ensuring that as few things as possible break. Often neglected, user interface elements must be designed, often the most difficult component as it will be the user's only contact point with the developer's work. The process is demanding, challenging and extraordinarily time intensive.

Legal processes, which differ from the development process in many respects, are now just as demanding and, in many ways, more critical to a developer's success than the code itself. The law, a discipline often thought of as cold and inflexible, is the anathema of the vibrant, expressive language of creativity, yet it haunts the software development process with a ghostlike presence. It can serve as a faithful partner or virulent opponent. In fact, truly successful apps, regardless of platform provider, share one remarkable commonality—each was born of a confluence of code and law. To put it simply, developers should view their apps as a "bundle" of technical and legal components.

And a rather large bundle it is, ranging from the contributions of individual programmers and designers to ownership values of the founders and shareholders, and much more. Business elements include such things as ownership of shares, the value of branding and experience and allocations of how revenue will flow. A variety of intellectual property comprises the core, a blend of copyrights, trademarks, confidential information, trade secrets and perhaps patents. A single app will contain multiple copyrights in the source and object code, graphical elements, user interface, design, music and sound effects, each of which have two distinct copyrights in the musical composition and corresponding sound recordings. There may be multiple trademarks as well, along with logos, branding and trade names or catchphrases. There will also be proprietary frameworks and libraries, each with their own copyright, and perhaps license rights. And do not forget the troll's favorite item of intellectual property—process (software) patents.

King's Candy Crush Saga, a particularly easy example given its ubiquity on devices around the world, and status as the most downloaded game in the history of Apple's App Store, has been successful not only because of its likability and high production value (design, gameplay, etc.) but because of its well executed branding and intellectual property strategy. A single concept spawned several an entire range of successful follow-ups across multiple platforms, based on the same fundamental concept. The real genius was the assimilation of the brand into popular culture and leveraging the value of that recognition to promote sequels in an extraordinarily unique way.

Similarly, Rovio's Angry Bird, which ranks a mere third in terms of all-time highest downloads, was a runaway success not because it was unique in any particular way. The creative and and whimsical gameplay, characters and mythology was used to develop a strong core brand which spawned an extraordinary number of successive hits. Additionally, Rovio masterfully excited an intellectual property licensing strategy that tied into major motion pictures, series shows and other forms of media including books and a range of merchandise. In short, it became quite the cultural phenomenon and still has relevance several years after its introduction. Without the law—proper entity structuring to hold the assets, intellectual property identification and strategy, licensing and cross-branding, brand development and all of the transactional elements that accompany those things, i.e. contracts, none of it would have been possible.

Developers must therefore do away with the typical view of the law and legal issues as a cost center. The euphemism has littered business school textbooks, seminars and other developer manuals and built a culture of fear and loathing surrounding legal issues. The problem with such a label is that it does not adequately describe the value of the fundamental system associated with the associated costs. And that system has certain rules and conditions associated with it that can make or break an indie app developer.

Again, the App Era exists primarily at the behest of the platform providers (Apple and Google). They are the gatekeepers. They are guarding the doors and holding all the keys. They own the infrastructure that transformed software delivery from the store shelf to the palm of the hand. Perhaps most importantly, they thrust indie and small developers to center stage with an audience of hundreds of millions of customers. During that revolutionary process, quietly and in the background, powerful forces amassed a dizzying array of intellectual property rights.

In fact, the extent of the intellectual property portfolios generated in the last decade is unlike anything in the history of the law. Most were not the result of talent and hard work but crafty drafting and a dose of good luck with a lazy patent examiner. Massive amounts of these broadly written patents were collected by those that could afford them. With them came an army of lawyers and number crunchers eyeing the prize--a gusher of money that would inevitably result. The law, its structures and processes were used very strategically by these investors to create a huge revenue potential. Developers must learn to act just as strategically if they wish to survive, let alone have a chance at being successful.

Survival.

Take a moment to think about that word, it's meaning and connotation. In the App Era, developers are adrift amidst a perfect storm of legal issues that can singlehandedly determine not only the success of their app but the continued existence of their business. To illustrate, there are countless disasters that result from improper business structure formation, lack of intellectual property protection and poorly written contracts, agreements and licenses. Further still, these problems can result in liability and potentially catastrophic costs at key growth points in the developer's business. Legal issues can also seriously affect, if not altogether destroy, financing, expansion or sales opportunities.

Most venture capitalists and finance minded folks have certain "qualifiers" they look for when they are considering an investment, particularly those dealing with software. The formula used may be based on personal or perhaps even eccentric criteria but one thing remains constant. There is a clear metric by which the product or company will be judged and, included in that, legal thresholds that will apply. Despite what is portrayed in popular media, money is not thrown at an enterprise without extensive due diligence (by lawyers) and strict adherence to standards.

Quite simply, a developer's use or misuse of legal processes and strategies may entirely determine an investment in their vision. Although deemed a cost center in the abstract world of business, law and legal principles are anything but that when money is on the line. In terms of financing, in particular, a developer that has taken the time and spent the money to integrate the law into their development process will be viewed by an investor as a more attractive investment. Likewise, proper use of legal strategy may save an indie developer from an unscrupulous investor looking for a quick and easy acquisition

Something as simple as the absence of a shareholder or partner agreement can make a potential investment target extremely unattractive.

This is because, whether it was considered important at the time or not, a problem will exist and need to be fixed, adding cost, time and unneeded complexity. Whatever investment is made, lingering problems will need to be addressed and fixing them—the process itself—detracts from the overall investment. Likewise, if there is an ownership issue regarding the intellectual property of a developer, the resulting legal time-bomb may prove too expensive or extravagant to warrant defusing.

Be assured that issues avoided at the formation of a developer's business have a perversely humorous way of showing up later when they are least welcome. The harsh reality of this statement underscores the conflict between coding and business mindsets. Developers simply want to make great stuff and find ways around anything that gets in the way. In other words, developers hack their way around problems. Lawyers, financiers and business people (the people in the suits) work through the problem to understand its nature and prefer to avoid it altogether.

To a developer, workarounds are a good thing—a method of getting something to work. In the practical world of app development, that is definitely a worthy goal. What works in the vacuum of code and compilers, however, will be regarded as a temporary fix from a legal perspective, where the goal is to thoroughly examine all options. Ideally, from a legal perceptive, it is preferred to avoid the problem so that it never arises again or at least not in the same way. In other words, the law wants a developer to plan for the best and prepare for the worst, something rarely discussed in the giddy throes of developer mania.

It cannot be stressed enough how important the above perspective is in the App Era, where one misstep can make or break a fledgling business.

Indeed, a fully integrated development process ultimately eliminates the notion of the legal cost center by embedding the law as part of the app coding process. In this environment, law and code function in harmony with one another, disparate elements of the same expression. Viewed in this context, the legal aspect of app development is anything but a frivolous cost.

BUSINESS STRUCTURES

THE SHELL GAME

Business structures are one of the most straightforward and practical legal devices a developer can use to protect their assets. Depending on the location in which the entity is formed, a legal business structure is relatively inexpensive and, with the right mindset, east to care for after formation. There are, however, differences between the various types of legal business structures that create a certain degree of choice depending on the circumstances. In selecting from among these, it is important to remember that there is no "perfect" choice. Each has strengths and weaknesses depending on the business, investment and other factors.

Having said that, there is a large contingent of solo and indie developers that share similar business and financial circumstances. Usually, these organizations are composed of one to five founders, some of whom may have money whereas others talent and sweat. More likely than not, smaller developers have either a single product in development or have just completed an app and are working on another. By and large, these groups tend to start with one coder forging an app of their own and ultimately needing others to keep growing.

In such cases, a simple corporation, partnership or hybrid entity will usually suffice for the company's asset and liability protection. The following information about each structure should give solo coders and indie developers a general idea of which is best in their particular circumstances. While professional advice may be necessary to register the entity with government officials and draft the formation documents, a working knowledge of the following investment vehicles will make the process much more efficient and pleasant for develops that are new to legal entities.

There are four general types of business structures:

Sole Proprietorships

Corporations

Partnerships

Hybrid Forms

Hybrids are unique in that they blend elements of corporations and partnerships for liability and legal purposes while accomplishing specific objectives for taxation. Although the above terms are for entity types in the United States, other countries have similar statutes regarding business entities, at least those where developers will most likely be setting up shop and doing business. Although the formalities, formation process and terminology may differ, most jurisdictions will have similar structures or at least an analogous option that produces the same legal results.

The business structures of the United States are used here as he terms have become quite popular in the business lexicon of the world. Secondly, the United States has been a hotbed of entity diversity due to the prevalence of lawsuits and the need to develop structures that limit a company's liability to damages. For better or worse, the laws of the United States, whether corporate, tax, intellectual property or otherwise, tend to influence or at least heavily overshadow the technology industry. At the very least, most develops will be releasing apps within the jurisdiction. So while specifics and practicalities differ, the types of entities discussed here are widely available.

Each entity and its principal advantages will be discussed in detail but it is crucial to understand the core reason legal business structures exist and their ultimate purpose. Primarily, legal or fictional entities developed as a way to functionally separate the business (and its assets) from the financial resources of the founders and shareholders. Particularly in the United States where lawsuits can involve millions of dollars in damages, the law evolved to allow the creation of an artificial "person"—the entity.

This entity acted as an avatar via which the founders and shareholders of the company could transact business. Because the entity's assets were limited to the total of its financial holdings, the company's owners were shielded in the event of a lawsuit. In other words, the legal entity limited the amount that debt collectors and others suing the company could collect solely to the entity's assets. The founders and owners were viewed as legal separate and safe.

Essentially then, a legal entity creates a border around a company to clearly mark where the business ends and the founders and owners begin. This is desirable for a variety of reasons, not the least of which is protection from liability, whether caused by financial obligations or legal claims and lawsuits. Except in very limited and exceedingly rare circumstances, a legal entity effectively exempts assets of the founders and owners from legal or financial claims against the company.

Most importantly for developers, the entity is considered a legally distinct "person" capable of owning, selling or transferring assets just as a living, breathing, flesh and blood human being does. The ramifications of this are huge and can be particularly strategic for intellectual property purposes. It fundamentally ensures that the company is free to use its resources in a singular capacity without consent from the specific individuals that created the asset. Imagine for a moment if a business continually had to ask for permission to use, transfer or license its properties. The creator of the asset would have an extreme advantage, especially in the case of important or highly valuable assets.

Legal entities solve that problem by allowing the company itself to own, manage and operate all of its property, intellectual or otherwise (copyrights, trademarks, patents, land, equipment, code, machinery, etc.) without asking for permission. This is perhaps the number one focus of investors and financiers that are contemplating investment in a company. Rights issues can be the major determining factor in investment discussions and must be treated seriously and with the utmost care.

While these issues may not appear essential during the early stages of a developer's life, the absolute worst scenario for a developer with an amazing app is to be hamstrung by rights to a particular property. Such issues severely impact a company's ability to maximize an app's commercial life. Why would an investor knowingly pour significant cash into a business that lacks complete control of its code, visual assets, UI, designs or logos? More often than not, these are the issues that complicate or completely ruin early stage financial negotiations with investors for indie and small developers.

To avoid such unfortunate circumstances, developers should beware the ghostly apparition of coders past and nail down the ownership of every single element in the app. And they should be able to prove it in writing. A simple rule to remember is that the continued viability of a company will be forever measured by ownership issues and what must be done to fix them.

That certainly sounds easy enough but ensuring that every asset, intellectual or otherwise, belongs one-hundred percent to the business is quite difficult. Moreover, obtaining written documents concerning that ownership is often extremely challenging. But, to put it simply—do the work. A developer must do whatever is necessary to document every aspect of asset ownership. They can rest assured that if there are lingering issues, they absolutely will be discovered during the due diligence phase of any investment process or, even worse, after the app launches.

This underscores a corollary rule that it is much easier, not to mention less expensive, to correct faults in new construction than in renovations. Companies are like buildings and, as time goes by, increasing wear and tear occur on internal structures. Whatever is ignored, from securing ownership rights to code written by a freelancer in New Delhi to the actual mechanics of the revenue split among founders, will eventually work their way to the surface. Like imperfections lying dormant in the foundation on which a house rests, such issues linger, only to be discovered when the stress finally overloads the frame.

Legal entities should therefore be thought of as the company's house wherein ideas, assets and money live. As with any construction, the foundation must be solid and capable of supporting the weight of what is built above. We will now examine each type of legal entity from that perspective. Once again, please note that comments about a particular entity should not be taken as an absolute. Each company is unique and the proper foundation for one may be a deathtrap for another.

A coder's goal should be to become familiar with the basic notion of separating business and personal assets, along with the ways in which the different entity types allow that to happen. Knowledge of the various available business structures will thereafter allow developers to make the most informed decision when it is time to make a choice.

THE ONE-PERSON SHOW

The simplest business form, the sole proprietorship is also the weakest in terms of asset and liability protection. The short summary is that there is absolutely no liability protection at all with this form of doing business. It is also the least useful in attracting financing and later growth. In fact, sole proprietorships are not really legal entities at all. It is the default form of business created merely by hanging up a shingle and selling a product or providing services.

While there may be a minimal registration requirement for a sole proprietorship, it is not formalized by it. In most jurisdictions, such a registration exists solely to have some record of a particular business name. In the software development context, a sole proprietor is usually an individual freelancer or solo coder that works for hire and does not choose to formalize their business by creating an entity. Doing so, however, places the entirety of the coder's personal assets at risk for debts and faults of the business.

In some jurisdictions, the Netherlands for instance, sole proprietors can register as such with the local government. Others, like the United States, only require registration of a sole proprietorship if the business uses a name other than the name of the individual selling the product or providing the service. There may also be certain industries that require registration of sole proprietors if the job function requires a business or technical license. Common in all these instances, however, is the idea that the individual is conducting the business directly. This distinctive feature makes the issue of liability extremely easy to answer.

Because there is no separation between the business and individual with the sole proprietorship, there is likewise no distinction between business and individual assets. All of a sole proprietor's personal financial resources can be used to satisfy debts and legal judgments from lawsuits arising from the business activity. This can be devastating to an indie coder or developer in the App Era where, as previously discussed, a handful of trolls own the bulk of functional and standards essential patents and intellectual property.

In such lawsuits, judgments can total in the millions, if not the hundreds of millions. Quite clearly, the sole proprietorship should not be considered a viable method of conducting business. It is mentioned here solely to inform the reader that if there is no formalized legal entity in place to protect the coder's business, this will be the potentially deadly default.

CORPORATIONS

Historically, most of the action in legal entities has been in the development of corporations. They are the de facto standard business entity in the United States and other jurisdictions around the world that have entity types closely aligned in principle. As we have discussed, an intangible shell into which assets are placed is highly desirable, as is the notion of limited liability. The corporation as a legal "person" is an idea that has allowed the law to accomplish both of those goals.

It is so ruthlessly effective at protecting founders and shareholders, it has grown exponentially since its inception to dominate modern business. With that ubiquity, it has also become a much maligned symbol for greed and avarice in free market capitalism. Such arguments aside, proper corporate structuring is an invaluable tool for coders competing in a world dominated by larger companies that have access to the best lawyers money can buy.

The corporate form is created by a particular jurisdiction's statute. In slightly less legal sounding terms, it is a product of government and exists only because a specific law authorizes it. Corporations are registered with state or national governmental agencies and sanctioned to conduct business as a living, breathing entity within that government's borders. Corporations have all the rights and privileges normally given to human beings, such as the ability to own property, enter into contracts, borrow money, etc. In the United States, regulation of corporations is a rather lackadaisical affair, whereas in other jurisdictions, they are very strictly monitored and controlled.

But if a corporation is fictional, yet recognized as a person, what makes up the corporation itself? At its core, a corporation is composed of a group of individual shareholders that acquire their shares in the company via an initial investment of money or services. The shareholders own their shares but do not officially represent the corporation on a day to day basis. That task is handled by the board of shareholder representatives, called directors, and director appointed managers, referred to officers. Directors govern at the highest level and the managers enforce decisions to form the basis of a functioning corporation.

The group of shareholder elected directors, called the board, is elected on an annual basis at the shareholders meeting. Even if there is only one shareholder, a "meeting" must still be held and recorded in writing in a log book called the "minutes." The directors also hold meetings and record their minutes but, unlike shareholders, can do much more in terms of wielding corporate power. Every large action of the corporation is usually voted on by the board and, in this way, the number and identity of the directors will play a key factor in how a corporation acts and what gets done. This is also the reason shareholders haggle over how many directors they may appoint.

One of the primary functions of directors is to elect officers, individuals that are accountable to the board for tasks such as accounting (the Chief Financial Officer), technology and infrastructure (the Chief Technology Officer), legal matters (the General Counsel) and, last but not least, principle executive decisions (the Chief Executive Officer).

Ideally, officers work together to create a harmonious blend of development and execution, although that is not often the case. Depending on the size of the company and the number of officers, the politics of who does and knows what often dictate the how and why of a particular conflict.

For indie coders and small developers, there will usually be one or a small group of shareholders, one or two directors and either a full staff of officers or, as is often the case, one officer that wears all the hats while trying to remain sane and upright. In these types of "closely held" corporations, there are specific legal rules on how minority shareholders, the ones that do not own as many shares as the others, are treated. Certain precautions must be taken to ensure that the interests of minority shareholders are preserved and protected and that they are generally not defrauded or dealt with unfairly.

Even smaller than the "closely held" corporations are the sole shareholder corporations. These companies are the no holidays, up all night, meat and potatoes indie coders. It may seem odd, but one individual can simultaneously be the only shareholder, the single director and the lone officer of a corporation. Although difficult to grasp initially, individuals can use the corporate form to effectuate exactly the type of legal strategy that is used by Fortune 500 companies. Rather than acting as a sole proprietor and being fully liable, an individual can use the corporate form and effectively cover their assets. Secondarily, the corporate form lends credibility and sophistication to small companies, especially when the time comes to start seeking outside investment.

Whatever the case may be, there are two types of corporate ownership at the shareholder level—private and public. Private corporations are owned solely by private shareholders who are usually restricted in how ownership of their ownership units in the company, called shares, may be sold. Public corporations, on the other hand, freely sell their shares via open markets called stock exchanges. Public companies are much more regulated than private companies, which enjoy a wide range of freedom in how they operate. If successful enough, a private corporation can register to sell its shares in the public exchanges in a process called an initial public offering, or IPO.

Whether private or public, the primary purpose of the corporate form is to distinguish business assets and liabilities from those of the individual shareholders. It is an incredibly useful legal device to separate the shareholders from activities of a business that is churning out products to the public, engaging in contractual relationships and, of course, borrowing money. Recall that with the sole proprietorship, the distinction between these activities simply does not exist. With the corporate form, the legal separation of the business persona and shareholders is elevated to an art form.

By detaching owners from the business and its activities, the corporate shell creates an extraordinarily powerful liability shield. If the company incurs a debt, only the assets of the corporation are legally at risk to pay the indebted amount. If there is a legal judgment against the corporation resulting from a lawsuit, only company owned assets are legally required to satisfy the judgment. And, despite popular euphemisms, the shield is quite difficult to break. There are very rare instances in which shareholders may be obligated to satisfy a corporate debt or judgment, most of which result from improper record keeping or, in all honesty, outright stupidity and/or brazen commingling of personal and business assets.

In addition to protecting shareholder assets from debts and liability, the corporate form also provides a useful container in which business assets can be held indefinitely, irrespective of shareholder lifespan. Think of a corporate entity as an armored vault, ready to be filled with all manner of things that it owns—tangible assets like equipment, intangible assets like intellectual property, contractual rights, licenses, real estate, buildings and any other thing under the sun that can be owned. Once those assets are in the vault, they are there indefinitely, unless the corporation is dissolved or wound up, of course. Unlike shareholders that eventually grow old and die, corporations are the Highlanders of the business world and can go on forever.

This can be quite useful in instances where those assets need to be shielded for particular reasons, such as protection from litigation that may affect an individual shareholder or in high-risk scenarios where future liability is difficult to assess or if ownership disputes suddenly arise. Such an arrangement also enables a corporation to license, or rent out, its properties for the duration of its useful life. We will discuss licensing in more detail later but, for now, it is important to note that licensing can be a very effective tool for software developers in many different scenarios and the corporate form is the perfect vehicle for doing so.

As an example, developers in Europe or Asia planning to release their app in the United States can create an American corporation that is owned entirely by its European or Asian counterpart. The American subsidiary is granted a license by the European company to distribute the app and functions merely as the releasing and distributing entity. The American company, however, does not own the app itself. In this scenario, lawsuits against the American entity are limited in their financial return for the suing party (usually a troll), making for a decidedly unattractive target. And because licenses can be granted and terminated at will, this arrangement can shift over time.

Recall that a corporation has a legal existence analogous to that of a living person and, as such, is able to own assets just a living, breathing human would. Unlike that of a warmblooded shareholder, however, corporate ownership is potentially infinite. A corporation can transfer, license or assign its rights in a property, as well as its obligations, to any other corporation in perpetuity. The ownership of a particular asset can therefore be strategically planned such that the core property is never truly at risk.

Aside from the obvious philosophical arguments relating to treating corporations as legal persons and the resulting shell game it enables, corporate protection can and should be used by developers. With proper planning, indie coders and developers can build a brand portfolio that is isolated from operating entities and any potential liability. Larger companies spend massive amounts on such things, sometimes using absurdly complex structures that take years, and hundreds of thousands of dollars, to fully implement. Indie coders and small developers can use those same tools.

PARTNERSHIPS

Like a corporation, a partnership is a collection of individuals conducting a specific business purpose. The principle difference between corporations and partnerships is tax related. Generally, corporations (as a singular "being" as viewed by the law) file their own tax return and pay their own tax, separate and in addition to taxes paid by shareholders. This is commonly referred to as "double taxation" and is the most cited criticism of the corporate form.

A partnership is viewed as a collective, rather than single "being" for tax purposes, with revenue flowing through the partnership to the partners individually. As a result, each individual partner files a separate tax return, while the partnership itself either does not file or files a minimal return solely for documentation purposes. This enables partnerships to avoid the double taxation seen with corporations and offer increased flexibility in the event the partners have different tax strategies or revenue goals.

Another difference between corporations and partnerships is the way profits are allocated among investors. In a corporation, each shareholder owns a number of shares proportionate to their investment interest. For example, if a shareholder purchases 100 shares from an available pool of 1,000 shares, that shareholder's ownership interest is 10% of the overall equity (value) of the company. In a partnership, however, the partners can agree to disproportionate ownership interests. For example, the partners can agree that although "Partner 1" invested only 5% of the overall equity,

"Partner 1" will nevertheless be entitled to 10%.

This the of flexibility in partnerships is extremely useful in instances where a developer wants to make certain concessions in order to secure valuable operating capital. A particular large investor may require a larger percentage of the overall return as a requirement for investing. And, in that case, a developer may wish to give larger piece of the pie. It is the business equivalent of the proverbial "carrot on a stick" and tends to work well in scenarios where comes at a price (as it usually does).

Despite its flexibility, there is one very large caveat when considering the partnership form. There are two different types of partnerships—general and limited. A general partnership can best be thought of as "group proprietorship" because, functionally, it is a sole proprietorship with simply more than one individual. And, just as with the sole proprietorship, a general partnership does not offer asset and liability protection to its partners. Legally, it is just a group of sole proprietors that happen to do business collectively.

A limited partnership, commonly referred to as an LP, is registered with a governmental authority and considered a legally distinct entity. It is made up of one general partner that operates the business day to day and a group of "limited" partners that are not actively involved in operations of the company. Limited partners are often referred to as "silent partners" and have full asset and liability protection, whereas the general partner does not. For this reason, when forming a limited partnership, a corporation or limited liability company (see below in hybrids) is appointed to act as the general partner.

To make things even more complex, there are also limited liability partnerships, referred to as LLPs, which eliminate the general partner requirement altogether. Therefore, in an LLP, all partners enjoy full asset and liability protection. The rest of this section will focus solely on LPs, as they are really the only viable choice for small develops wishing to create a partnership. LLPs are exorbitantly expensive and typically used in complex scenarios, none of which relate to the core audience of this book, at least in the initial stages of their business. Still, even an LP is more expensive and complex to form than a corporation.

The higher expense is primarily due to the difference in tax treatment. Also, government registration fees for LPs tend to be higher than corporations, mostly to ensure that only those with sufficiently "sophisticated" business constructions are able to form them.   The "LP" designation indeed reeks of snobbery and those that choose them tend to fully grasp the aura and mystique exuded by those two magical letters. Secondarily, the agreement that governs the relationship between partners is usually much more complex than the typical corporate shareholder agreement. Again, this is primarily due to the tax issues and the fact that partnership interests can be allocated disproportionately.

As mentioned above, there are two types of partners in an LP, a general partner and usually a number of limited partners. Limited partners are essentially corporate shareholders and directors combined and have absolute limited liability. They cannot be held responsible for corporate debts or legal judgments. The general partner, and every LP must have at least one, acts in the same capacity as the chief executive officer and carries out the day to day business of the company. As a result, the general partner is exposed to full personal liability for all actions. This unique quirk of LPs is the reason that most general partners are corporate entities (see below).

The different in general and limited partners is rooted in the typical financial condition of the partners themselves. The limited or so-called "silent partners" are typically folks with a load of cash to invest in the business and merely want a return on that investment. Limited partners are exactly that—limited. They have no right to act on behalf of the partnership in any way or be active in day to day management or operations. The general partner, on the other hand, has full authority to act on behalf of the partnership and coordinates all operational activities. The general partner can sign contracts, take out loans and do whatever is necessary to run the company. Because of such absolute discretion, however, the general partner is personally liable.

With LPs, there is always at least one partner that assumes the full risk of the business and acts as the general partner. Typically, this position was relegated to the partner that made the least significant financial contribution, the "sweat equity" partner, who had little to lost in the first place. Still, it seems rather draconian to subject the poor workaday grunt that shoulders the running of the company to full liability, doesn't it?

General partners that put some coin in their pocket only to lose it because of the liability exposure felt much the same. Resulting, they hired lawyers and developed a rather novel solution to protect the pitiful soul that was to be appointed general partner and be completely on the hook. The answer came in the form of an existing legal framework—the corporation. Because it is a legal "person," a corporate entity is perfectly capable of serving as the general partner in an LP, thus affording the individual toiling for partnership profits the same liability protection given to the limited partners.

A developer unlucky enough to be in the line of fire may simply form a corporate entity, with themselves as the sole shareholder and director, and designate that corporation as the general partner. Thus, the entirety of the LP is fully protected from liability, including the developer. If, for instance, there is a lawsuit against the corporate general partner, only the assets of that corporate entity are at stake to satisfy the legal judgment that results. Of course, if proper planning has been done, no assets are actually held by the corporate general partner and any resulting liability is therefore zero.

Necessity, they say, is the mother of invention.

HYBRIDS

Following the development of corporations and LPs, business owners and investors were forced to choose between the two entity types depending on various tax and equity considerations. There were often various tradeoffs depending on the goals or requirements of the business setup. As an answer to this dilemma, creative lawyers in Texas (where everything is bigger) developed the idea of the limited liability company, or LLC, a unique and specialized entity that combined the best parts of the corporation with the soothing, jazzy tax elements of the LP, all the while offering limited liability to all those involved.

In an LLC, taxes flow through to each individual investor, just like in a partnership. And, also like partnerships, ownerships values can be disproportionate to relative investment. But perhaps most important to indie coders and small developers, the documentation requirements are significantly reduced. For instance, rather than holding a yearly shareholder meeting to elect directors, who then elect officers, an LLC's structure can be designated once in the operating agreement between the members (LLC speak for shareholders) and then put aside.

This is extremely advantageous for smaller organizations from an administration perspective. At the inception of the company, an LLC may designate a particular individual to be in charge of a particular function until further notice. And that's it. There are no additional meetings to have and no further elections to be made and documented. No corporate books or binders are required, along with the mountains of paperwork. A company may simply say, "This is our champion," and let it ride.

Such flexibility is ideal for an indie coder or small organization. In those environments, complying with the documentation requirements of the corporate form can be extraordinarily burdensome. More often than not, administration is swept under the rug and simply forgotten. Likewise, LPs are expensive and much more complex, requiring a lengthy, i.e. costly, partnership agreement that may take several months to generate. In comparison, LLCs are so easy to form and administrate that they are an excellent choice when an indie coder or small development developer wants to "set it and forget it." Like a background process, an LLC can be a silent, yet extremely valuable tool in a coder's business operations.

WHY THIS STUFF MATTERS

Why do business structures matter to a coder? The short and simple answer is that they can save an app's life. The term "life" is meant here in its broadest sense—legal business entities protect apps (and their creators) from being destroyed if the proverbial shit hits the fan. There is simply no substitute for the legal barrier a carefully selected entity creates around an app and its assets. It is something that is extremely difficult to break through or tear down once constructed. Moreover, the damage that can result from its absence is nearly impossible to repair.

To quote my grandfather, one of the wisest men I have ever known, "It's a helluva lot better to have it and not need it than need it and not have it."

Along with effective protection for a coder's app and business assets, a formal business structure provides a single repository for intellectual assets. This is important for many reasons, not the least of which is to make sure that all intellectual property contained in the app is properly owned by the business, either by creation or licensing. This ensures that intellectual assets may be sold, transferred or licensed freely by the company and provides security that is crucial for potential investment and growth.

For example, the business must be able to demonstrate to potential investors that it fully owns, or is licensed to use, what it intends to sell. Without that, an investor would be asked to buy into a product or company whose foundation may be subject to ownership disputes regarding core assets. Imagine a developer's star app, created by a team of freelancers, without any written agreements reciting it is a work for hire. While it may seem trivial on the surface, this scenario would most certainly grind investment negotiations to a definitive halt.

The above example illustrates the profound importance of consolidating (or, in a sense, "compiling") business assets into a single vessel— a legal entity with potentially indefinite existence (the "executable" if the example is carried further). A developer must treat their business like the apps they create—a valuable bundle of bits, resources, assets and properties. That bundle—a well constructed shell, be it a corporation, partnership or LLC—is the key to a developer's financial success and legal security.

Where that bundle is located—the legal location of

a business structure—is often an afterthought. More often than not, business owners assume that the best place to formally structure their business is wherever they live or work. In many cases, this may ultimately be the best choice but there are many issues that should be considered before that decision is made. Additionally, it is not uncommon to create multiple business structures for purposes of segregating assets, intellectual or otherwise, to protect against potential liability.

For example, European developers routinely release their products in the United States via the localized app stores supplied by their platform provider. In the App Era, as we have discussed, troll are lying in wait to assert various, and often ridiculous, legal claims against a popular app or a new developer. Trolls are a significant threat to developers and the technology sector altogether, particularly in the United States where litigation has become a lucrative business model. In this type of hostile environment, multiple business structures are a powerful, albeit complex, defensive strategy.

The theory behind such a design is simple—hide the money. It works mostly because typical trolls will drop a line of inquiry or assertion of rights if no money to be made from the process. Obsessively profit driven, trolls are far more focused on money to be made from doing nothing at all rather than contributing to industry. That said, if a troll gets even the faintest whiff of a coder's profits, even those to be generated in the future, rest assured they are at risk.

Even though trolls were once viewed as a lethargic blight on the industry, they have increasingly displayed a willingness to attack even the smallest businesses in the pursuit of profit. If a developer implements a multiple entity structure, however, a company's assets and profits may be obfuscated and hidden from view. This is not the mere academic exercise it seems. The core of any developer's business is intellectual property and, for trolls, that is just another revenue stream waiting to be exploited. The greater the distance a a developer can put between its intellectual property and the grubby little hands of potential litigants, the better.

In the typical scenario, a business structure outside of the United States serves as the primary company and owns all intellectual property. An entity in the United States is created for entrance into the app stores and holds a license granted by the "offshore" company to use and distribute the app. In the event of an infringement lawsuit, the troll will immediately perceive that the process of asserting its claims will be more difficult and, depending on the structure implemented, potentially worth nothing. The US entity merely owns a license, an asset inherently worth less than the licensed asset.

By playing this "shell game," the motivation for a troll, or any potential litigant for that matter, decreases significantly. From a plaintiff's attorney perspective, even the most salivating set of facts are worthless if there is next to zero possibility of collecting actual cash against any judgment obtained. Of course, lawsuits could also be filed against offshore entities but to do so requires a massive amount of time and money. Unless the potential return is exceptionally large, the burden far outweighs the return. Thus, even the simplest multiple entity structure can provide significant protection for a small developer or indie coder.

Likewise, business structures not only protect the company from outside interference, but also protect the founders and owners from themselves. Development firms are usually firmed by friends or colleagues that have no reason (at least during formation) to question each other's integrity. Such implicit trust is truly a remarkable thing to have and, if you have it, you are very lucky indeed. However, it has been my experience that, when money and ownership enters the equation, there is a propensity for human behavior to radically change, usually for the worse.

Still, most founders begin their relationship thinking, "There is nothing to fight over right now." While this may be accurate at the earliest stages of a company's operations, it usually does not remain so for very long. As soon as development begins, intellectual property is necessarily created and there must be a creator, an owner to whom the value of the creation belongs. It is shortly after this point where things fall apart from a human behavior perspective, especially when the core issues of ownership, attribution and payback remain unaddressed. Formalizing the business structure gives authenticity and meaning to everything that occurs during development. And it can save a relationship in the process.

For instance, if there are disputes about to whom an idea belongs or "who came up with what," a business structure and its agreements provide a definitive answer. Without the clarity of written expression, all answers are mere speculation until proven and, even then, it may not matter at all.

Some issues, such as the transfer of intellectual property rights, are valid only when in writing (see below). If there is no formal structure to hold the ownership of intellectual assets and no documents evidencing that intent, the issue is moot—whoever created the asset owns it. This, of course, creates an overabundance of fear, uncertainty and doubt.

Aside from the obvious disputes that arise between founders, owners, contractors and employees in such situations, the real conflict develops between the company and its brand. Successful brands are a carefully crafted, artistic mixture of vision and execution. Ownership disputes over intellectual property, revenue sharing and payouts cloud vision and bring execution to a standstill. The product suffers, not only in quality but in the nature of the thing itself—it was never given the chance to fully be what it could have been. Instead, it was mired in a series of petty disputes, squabbles and pissing matches.

A truly great product results from a well-oiled machine, hell-bent on making something genuine and to the fullest degree. A properly structured business is absolutely vital to that machinery.

SUMMARY

Formal business structures provide convenient, secure containers in which business assets may be kept. Doing so allows a company's founders and owners to protect personal assets against attacks against the business. Collecting business assets in a single entity also allows for unencumbered use of intellectual property by a single owner with a potentially unlimited lifespan. In other words, legal entities confirm physical and intellectual assets for business operations. Additionally, centralizing ownership provides a sound foundation for future investment by assuring investors that assets are properly owned and managed by one entity—the company.

Business structures also secure founders and owners against potential litigation in foreign markets. Shielding the entity that owns a company's intellectual property by licensing distribution rights to a foreign subsidiary is an excellent deterrent to litigation, especially from trolls. At the very least, multiple entity structures provide yet another hurdle over which potential litigants must leap to get to the money. And that extra little bit of difficulty may be the determining factor in the decision to sue.

Perhaps most importantly, however, business structures help to prevent the most destructive type of disputes—those between founders or owners. With a defined ownership structure and formalized rules regarding revenue and payouts, many issues can be resolved before fighting even begins. Generally speaking, if there is a playbook to follow, most people tend to follow it. This kind of knowledge does more than place restrictions on what can and cannot be done. It defines a place for each founder, owner and contributing individual, informing them of their various rights and acts as a silent advisor regarding which battles are worth fighting. Indeed, the mere act of formalizing a business structure with a legal entity can save founders and owners from vicious in-fighting that distracts the business from its purpose.

This leads to the most crucial take-away of all: the type of business structure chosen is not as important as the simple act of choosing one in the first place. Coders and their businesses are as richly varied as the apps they create, so much so that the "right" choice for one could be the "wrong" choice for another. More pivotal than what form is selected is that developers know there are choices, investigate those choices and analyze their business to leverage the available options. The analytical process itself is the goal, rather than making a "perfect" choice.

The value of the process is too great to be calculated in the traditional sense. The more familiar a coder becomes with their own unique circumstances, the deeper the understanding of the effect of those conditions on their business. That, more than any specific legal or programming tool, is critical to enabling a developer to do what they do best—making great apps.

INTELLECTUAL PROPERTY

THE GHOST IN THE MACHINE

Of all the things in the App Era about which developers are most often concerned, intellectual property stands at the forefront. "What exactly is it?" "Do I have any and, if so, what do I do with it?" These are the types of questions most often asked about intellectual property. The first is the most easy to answer but significantly less important than the second. But there is a third question relating to intellectual property that developers should be asking but usually do not.

Before revealing that question, it is important to have a general understanding of what intellectual property is, its purpose and how it is generally used in the context of coding software. By nature, developers tend to be goal oriented. Such an attitude is hugely beneficial when it comes to the arduous task of conceptualizing, programming, debugging and finalizing an app.

The first very important thing to grasp about intellectual property is that it exists from the moment an asset is created (or, in the case of trademarks, used in commercial activities) and continues to acquire value thereafter. When that notion is applied to coding, the idea of an app as a result of a process shifts to that of a bundle of rights—a package consisting not only of code and resources but also legal rights and business value.

There are many types of intellectual property included in that bundle of rights. The first, and most immediately valuable in the coding context, is copyright, which protects the code, written materials, graphical elements and all other media that makes up the app. Secondly, there are trademarks—logos, band names, titles and other elements developed for the app and the developer's company or trade name. Third, there can be contractual license rights relating to materials used or produced in the creation of the app. Fourth, the app may be so novel and unique that it contains patentable elements, although software patents are perhaps the most hotly contested area of intellectual property. Finally, there are "non-statutory" forms of intellectual property, such as trade secrets, confidential information and otherwise unregistered intellectual assets.

We will examine each of the types of intellectual property in detail. Perhaps most importantly, we will discuss the value and application of each type in terms of the development process and the resulting app. As we discuss each type of intellectual property, maintain the view of the finished product as a bundle of rights, with each type of right in the bundle contributing to the overall value of the whole.

COPYRIGHT

Copyright protects the *expression* of ideas and imbues ownership of that expression to its creator. That is, whenever a painter paints, a sculptor sculpts or a writer writes, the resulting work may only be copied, distributed or used with the creator's written permission. That broad power is what gives copyright its name—the creator of a work has the sole and exclusive right to copy it. In addition to protecting creative expression from unauthorized reproduction, there are other rights granted to the creator that hold just as much commercial value.

The five exclusive rights of copyright are as follows: 1) the right to reproduce, 2) the right prepare derivative works (e.g. sequels, adaptations, etc.), 3) the right to distribute copies,

4) the right to perform the work and 5) the right to display the work. Each right is separate and gives rise to an independent legal cause of action in the event of infringement. For instance, in one act of copyright infringement, there may be a reproduction made, from which a derivative work is crafted, which is then distributed and/or displayed.

All of these rights overlap to form a layer of protection around a software product. The right to reproduce an app is the most visible sign of infringement and, incidentally, the most easily quantified. Unauthorized copies can be readily seen and evoke much anger and resentment from coders. Yet, the act of reproduction itself, as voluminous as it may be, is but one spoke in the wheel of copyright's protective power.

Derivative works, adaptations or modifications of

the original work usually accompany any work that has been reproduced without permission. In the age of DRM and activation schemes, modifying or "cracking" an app such that it functions outside of its original app store purchase or without activation creates a derivative work. That is, the original app is revised in such a transformative way that it becomes an entirely new app, as copyright is concerned. Things such as film sequels, an installment of a book series or unauthorized mix of a song are also examples of derivative works.

The power to control the creation of such works is critical. Otherwise, apps are susceptible to cracking or spawning knock-off apps based on the original. Further, the power to prohibit derivative works also protects web sites, advertising/marketing copy and other commercial materials. In some cases, the copyright for these materials may even be more critical than the copyright for the app itself.

For example, imagine a website advertising a coder's app that is copied transformed ever-so-slightly to suit the needs of a competitor. Usually, this is done by making a copy of the original from which to work and creating a derivative work for a separate purpose. Once the derivative website is published, the unauthorized use includes infringement of the exclusive rights to reproduce, prepare derivative works, and to distribute and display the work. This example illustrates the spiritual core of copyright—to protect how creative expression is delivered to the public.

In the context of apps, distribution to the public is a key component of a solid copyright protection strategy. This is where platform providers prove incredibly useful. If the sole source for an app is its respective app store, and if a customer must have a valid and operational account for that store in order to gain access, developers are at least assured that their creation is being distributed properly. However, it is possible for apps to be reproduced and distributed after they are purchased. Although such instances usually require cracking, which creates a derivative work, they are becoming more frequent.

The goal of this line of examples is public performance or display. These two rights are parallel with one another, merely differing in the type of work they protect. The right to perform publicly covers the public performance of literary, musical, dramatic, choreographic, pantomime, audio-visual and motion pictures works. The term "public" means performance of the work in a place open to the public or where a a group of people who are not family or social acquaintances might gather. Also protected is performing the copyrighted work at multiple locations simultaneously, as is the case with streaming audio or video feeds.

This right applies to apps generally, since they are considered literary works for purposes of copyright. Most software can also be classified as an audio-visual work these days, owing to the inclusion of graphical, visual and audio elements that make up modern apps. Nonetheless, this area of law is still developing, though it would certainly apply to software that requires, by its nature, performance at multiple locations, such as multi-player and network accessible games or social media apps.

Similarly, the right to publicly display protects literary, musical, dramatic, choreographic, pantomime, pictorial, graphical, sculptural and still image works. The scope of protection and definition of "public" are the same as with the right to publicly perform. The single differentiating factor is the type of work subject to protection. The law has merely evolved to conceptualize a sculptural or pictorial work to be "displayed" rather than "performed." For purposes of this book, the distinction merely highlights the type of work.

It is important to note that an underlying requirement to any of the preceding rights is that the work be "fixed" in some sort of tangible medium. In other words, the work must be reside on or in a physical substance such that it is perceptible by others. It would be rather impossible to prevent others from copying what is in one's mind and, thus, copyright does not claim to protect ideas of what one wishes to express. Indeed, copyright exists as motivation to move those ideas out of a creator's mind and into the world.

The exact tangible medium is immaterial, as long as it is capable of storing and, thus, transmitting the work in physical space. Paper, stone, vinyl records, magnetic tape, pits on a compact disc, digital data on a hard drive platter or solid state chip—any of these will suffice. Again, copyright encourages creators to carve their inspired thoughts into a readily observable, or at least decipherable, mechanism rather than maintain a swirl of ideas locked inside a creative mind.

Part of that goal stems from the difficulty in

protecting abstract ideas, which are subject to the whims and fancy of the individual. Secondarily, fixing the work in a tangible medium allows the public to enjoy the expression of the idea. This artistic encouragement is tempered by the resulting protection for the creator. As creative thoughts are exposed to the public, copyright confers a commercial benefit to creators by prohibiting others from using and profiting from the expression. Otherwise, content creators would find their works exploited by others, a scenario that sometimes happens even with the protection of copyright. If this were the default, the motivation to create would be greatly diminished, thereby reducing the overall creative inventory.

The core of copyright's power is the bargaining capacity it gives an author from the very moment that the material is tangibly fixed. Think about it—

no one else in the universe can use that material in any commercial way, without permission, for a fixed amount of years. That is a very strong position, especially given the extremely long copyright terms currently in effect. Although there are different terms depending on the type of work and its creation or publication date, consider that a published work presently enjoys a copyright term of 70 years following the death of creator. Further consider that if we are talking about a work of corporate authorship, the term is 95 years following publication or 120 years following the date of creation, whichever expires first.

The fact that a corporate author, as owner of a work for hire produced by a contractor, enjoys a copyright term of 95 years following publication or 120 years following the date of creation underscores the nexus of business structures and intellectual property. Large companies have lobbied for the development of these ideas and have used them to secure powerful market positions. Yet even an indie coder can use the same strategy to lock down their software with the power of copyright.

For example, if a developer codes a clever new physics engine, only that developer is able to profit from it. If another unscrupulous company copies portions of the code to craft a competing product, the original developer can stop the use of the code and be reimbursed for profits are gained by its unauthorized use. This ability to demand and collect monetary damages for unauthorized use is an incredibly powerful tool in the App Era.

Generally speaking, however, if someone wants to copy something, they will simply do it. The prohibition of copyright is unlikely to deter everyone from copying or using the material—movie and music piracy being an excellent example of that fact. Aside from mere copying for personal use, there are others that snag a copyrighted work and use it for their own commercial benefit. Coders should be concerned with both, as the former repents lost sales and the latter is the siphoning of revenue and years of valuable creative labor.

Copyright, however, is more than a mere "DO NOT COPY!" sign on the gate. Recall that copyright vests complete and total ownership of a material in its creator. This means that any profits resulting from the work are legally owned by the creator. In the event that the work is copied, distributed or used in such a way that it generates revenue, copyright allows the creator to step in an recover those revenues and potentially much, much more.

When a work is used without the permission of the copyright holder, damages will likely be generated. That is, if code is copied and used commercially, some amount of money will be generated from it. By all accounts, the original developer can request that the exact amount of financial gain from the unauthorized use be returned. However, most copyright statutes allow for the concept of "statutory damages," which are amounts fixed by the law and must be paid to the content creator, regardless of the actual amount of damages suffered. There are requirements that must be met to seek statutory damages, like the registration of the work with the applicable copyright office prior to infringement or unauthorized use. Relatively speaking, though, these requirements are a small burden when examining the potential return from the damages amount set by law.

For instance, in the United States, statutory damages are allowed to be granted by a court, in its discretion according to the facts of the case, at the rate of $750 to $30,000 per work. In the event that the infringement was committed "willfully" (it was known that the work was copyrighted and the infringer acted regardless), the statutory damages amount can be increased up to $150,000 per work. Given the nature of copying and the number of specific acts of infringement that can be involved, it is entirely possible that one act of infringement can involve statutory damages upwards of $1,000,000. Such stratospheric amounts are a very useful bargaining tool when threatening or conducting litigation against someone who has infringed a copyrighted work.

In preventing the copying or use of a work, copyright serves as the basis for one of the most productive and economically practical tools in software—the license. Rather than locking the ability to copy and use code to themselves, a developer may choose to license all or a portion of a particular work in order to better exploit its commercial potential. For instance, if a developer develops a framework for a game, that framework can be licensed to others who may not have the ability to code it themselves, for economic or other reasons. Licensing can create multiple revenue streams for a developer, even if that possibility was not a firsthand consideration. It is for this reason that developers must examine their business and fully integrate intellectual property and law as necessary frameworks in the development process.

Licensing can be beneficial even when it is not outgoing. That is, a developer can also benefit economically from an inbound license—when a developer licenses something from another source. In the above example, the developer without sufficient resources to develop a particular framework for a game licenses the software from its original author. In that instance, development hours and a great deal of money are saved. Essentially, rather than "reinventing the wheel," the wheel is simply licensed from another source. This methodology has several advantages, especially when looking at reproducible elements such as frameworks, engines, interfaces and items that are used again and again.

Licensing is crucial to the App Era.

After all, it is a license of various frameworks and APIs that enables developers to code for the mobile platform providers in the first place. Apple, for example, requires that developers enroll in the iOS Developer Program to access the resources, frameworks, APIs and documentation necessary to produce an iOS app. It would be impossible to do so otherwise, because of the sheer volume of reproducible elements and functions that are supplied by the platform providers. Without licensing, app development, in and of itself, would be an incredibly expensive and time-consuming endeavor.

Licensing will be discussed in more detail below but, for now, it is sufficient to note that it is a robust mechanism capable of reducing the barrier to entry for certain programmatic elements. Additionally, licensing enables a developer to commercially exploit otherwise untapped revenue. The focus, then, should be on the overall value of the code, the intellectual property that has been created, rather than the value of the app itself. Copyright and licensing are the magical elixir that make that possible.

TRADEMARKS

At their core, trademarks are not a mere protection mechanism. Rather, trademarks are words, phrases or symbols that designate the source of origin of a particular product. In other words, a trademark is how a business "stamps" its product such that customers can easily find the product again in the marketplace. Brand names ("Apple"), sport team mascots ("Dallas Cowboys"), logos (Apple's bitten apple logo), distinctive shapes (the original Coca-Cola bottle) and catchphrases ("Think Different") are all ways that a company tries to single out its brand from the others on the market.

Additionally, companies use trademarks to identify particular products within their overall brand. For example, Apple has spent considerable time and expense building up the visibility and value of the

"Apple" brand and the bitten apple logo that accompanies it. Further still, the company has identified products sold by that brand with other trademarks such as "MacBook Pro," "iPhone," "iPad" and "QuickTime" (including the fanciful "Q" shaped icon). All of these things differentiate Apple's products as "brands" that can be repeatedly sought out for the same experience, performance, characteristics and design. Yet, separate and distinct from the product brands themselves, the "Apple" brand represents the source from which the products came. This is why companies usually refer to products by both the company and product brands, such as "Apple iPhone" or "Apple MacBook Pro."

Again, the chief function of all this branding is to help customers identify the source of a product. Without it, the marketplace is an unkempt sea of knock-offs and lookalikes that confuse and mislead customers into making purchases of items from an unknown source. Trademarks help avoid this problem by allowing businesses to tap into the human ability to recognize distinctive images, words, phrases and symbols and repeat a buying pattern that produces satisfaction and familiarity. Essentially, trademarks allow a company to distinguish its products on an overcrowded shelf and allow consumers to make a decision based on their previous brand experience. The core function of a trademark, then, is to create a strong association between source and product.

Such an association builds up over time in a customer's mind and is quantified with the concept of "goodwill." The term refers to the collective "shine" that has accumulated on the company and its brand based on customers' repeated purchases and satisfaction. If a trademarked product satisfies customers, it is likely they will repeat the purchase in the future. Thus, the trademark creates a bond between company and customer based on trust.

The confidence generated by the trademark, in turn, propels the customer to buy more of the same thing from the same source. Moreover, the strength of that bond increases the power of the trademark to both pull in repeat customers and create new sales. Repeat customers want the brand experience again, whereas new sales result from the "halo of awesomeness" that surround the trademark. Repeat customers consistently purchase and talk about the brand, and therefore the company, contributing to the halo and overall perception of the brand.

In some instances, it is possible for things that are

not necessarily words, phrases or symbols to receive trademark protection. The Coca-Cola bottle, for example, is merely a particular bottle shape yet it enjoys trademark protection. However, with these types of marks, it is generally required that the "feature" not provide any functional or competitive advantage to the product. In other words, the Coca-Cola bottle shape is a trademark because it allows customers to recognize that a particular bottle is a Coca-Cola, rather than performing any specific function in containing the beverage inside. Otherwise, features that give a functional or competitive advantage are generally protected under the legal concept of "trade dress," which we will discuss in more detail below.

It is worth noting that there is a dark side to the goodwill that built up around a trademark. As the trademark gains significance and luster in the minds of customers, competitors are more likely to attempt the same manner of branding or "hitch a ride" on the popularity of the mark. This results in competing trademarks trying to associate themselves with or mimic well established brands. A classic example of this scenario developed when every competitor to Apple's iPad began naming their tablets "[something]pad" or "I[something]". This type of competition blurs the association between company and product, directly interfering with the goodwill that has developed around a particular brand.

The potential loss of association between a company and its mark leads to the most common type of trademark dispute, in which one company claims that another's trademark is "confusingly similar" to its own. The circumstances can vary wildly but, at its core, there is use of a trademark that is likely to cause confusion among customers as to the source of the products being sold or the sponsorship or approval of the product. For example, a company may produce a tablet designed to compete with Apple's iPad with the name "HiPad."

In this admittedly obvious example, a customer who is familiar with Apple and its trademarked "iPad" brand may be confused as to which is which. Alternatively, customers may believe that Apple is, in some way, sponsoring or approving the alternative product. Another example would be a company selling an accessory and, as part of the advertising, Apple or iPad trademarks are prominently displayed. A customer may suspect that Apple is endorsing or somehow approving the particular product and be confused.

Using a brand name that is confusingly similar to another would yield similar results. For instance, a computer and electronics company called "Applets" would be confusingly similar to "Apple" and thus give rise to trademark infringement. It is important to note, however, that the industries and products must somehow overlap. Therefore, a car rental company called "Apple Leasing" would be perfectly acceptable, as there is little danger of one being confused for the other. The fundamental premise is that trademarks should not be used in such a way that creates confusion, because the ultimate goal is to distinguish products and their producers.

However, companies can use trademarks in ways that do not confuse yet are still infringing. Recall that the cumulative value of the "shine" attached to a trademark resulting from the positive associations between the brand and the product is called goodwill. It encompasses the reputation of a company and is, therefore, critical to maintain. Once the trademark becomes sufficiently famous, negative associations can blur or tarnish the mark in the minds of customers. Although resulting from different circumstances, the end result is the same —the trademark loses its shine and, thus, some of its value.

Blurring results when a well-known trademark is weakened by an association with dissimilar products. For example, Apple branded lights reduce the associative power between Apple, the computer and electronics company, and their products. This results because the trademark is so well-known for technology related items, that the use of the mark with regard to other goods causes a rift in customer attitudes and thinking about the brand. At the very least, the impact of the famous trademark is diminished because of the softer, weaker trademark that deals with dissimilar goods.

Likewise, using a trademark in an unflattering or negative way has a similar effect. Here, the brand loses value not because of a weaker trademark attached to dissimilar goods but through an association with inappropriate or improper goods. With the rise of the Internet, the potential for tarnishment is quite great. For instance, a pornographic website whose domain name is apple.xxx would weaken the value of the "Apple" trademark because it attempts to associate "Apple" with pornographic material. In a sense, the "bad reputation" of the one becomes attached to the other merely by association. Although seemingly prudish, tarnishment of a trademark is an extremely sensitive matter to a brand. As such, care must be taken to protect the trademark against unsuitable associations, no matter how slight

There are, of course, other causes of action that can potential arise in a trademark infringement claim. However, most are based on common law concepts of unfair competition and exceed the scope of this book. One worth mentioning is "passing off," the practice of attempting to sell a product as if it were made by another company or brand. For example, manufacturing an iMac lookalike and subsequently slapping an Apple logo on the side of the box is passing off at its finest. Conversely, taking a computer made by Apple, stripping off the Apple logo and adding a different trademark to make it appear as if another brand produced it is referred to as "reverse passing off."

All of these examples have used "Apple," a wildly famous trademark, with the point being that Apple would bring down the legal hammer to protect its valuable brand. However, even indie and small developers benefit from the protection of trademark. It ensures that, at the end of the day, customers who purchase a particular product know what they are getting and where they can get it again.

To use another famous example, one can go to Katmandu, order a Big Mac and expect to receive the same Big Mac they received in Portland three weeks before. For a developer, this consistent association of high quality with a particular product is crucial to success. In the App Era, the shelves are as crowded as ever. In order to standout in a

Technicolor explosion of icons and product descriptions, it is pivotal to develop a positive brand image to let customers know where to go when they want great stuff.

To do this, a developer need nothing more than a creative and consistent approach to branding. The very second that a word, symbol or phrase is used in commerce, it is a trademark. That is, from the time it is first used in a commercial capacity, the trademark starts to accrue value as a brand. a developer can complete the brand with the "™" symbol beside the name as soon as it is first used in commerce. There are, however, certain benefits of registering the trademark, primarily a governmentally sanctioned presumption of validity for the trademark. In other words, once a trademark is registered, it is much more difficult for it to be claimed invalid. Additionally, a developer can use the "®" symbol beside the trademark once registered, lending even more legitimacy to the trademark.

As with everything else, however, there are certain rules for the registration of trademarks. First and foremost, the proposed trademark must, in fact, be capable of designating the origin or source. That is, it cannot be confusingly similar to any trademark already registered ("Apple Phones"), nor can it be a generic term ("Blanket"), a surname ("Kennedy Apps"), a term merely describing the geography from where the product comes ("Italian Apps") or a variety of other complex exclusions. The point here is that the trademark must be sufficiently "whimsical" enough to stand out from ordinary language.

The strength of a trademark is generally

determined by an analysis of how creative or thought provoking the trademark potentially is. Remember, the ultimate goal is to differentiate a particular product or brand from another. The more generic, merely descriptive or bland the trademark, the less distinctive and, therefore, less differentiating it is.

The strongest trademarks are the ones that are fanciful or arbitrary because the law views them as being inherently distinctive An example of such a trademark is "Colorblind Sasquatch" for extremely durable leather messenger bags. The trademark itself "stands out" by being distinctive in and of itself. A "suggestive" trademark such as "Tuff & Bullish," although weaker, is still a potentially registrable trademark because it suggests, rather than merely describing, the qualities and characteristics of the product.

Weak marks, on the other hand, tend to describe the product or are the generic words for the product itself. For example, "World's Best Apps" is not a strong trademark for a developer to use because it merely describes what the products are intended to be. On the other hand, if a developer can demonstrate that such a descriptive trademark has acquired "secondary meaning" then the trademark would be registrable. Generally, secondary meaning is shown by surveys and questionnaires given to customers. As a result, it is a time-consuming and expensive method.

Generic terms can never acquire secondary meaning and are therefore completely barred from being registered as trademarks. The reason for this is so that generic terms are not capable of being commandeered by companies for commercial purposes. Conversely, a registered trademark is capable of becoming a generic term and losing its status as registered. This process results when a very well-known mark is used to generically describe the article itself.

The best-known example is Thermos, a once famous trademark that became the de facto generic term for an insulated cylinder capable of maintaining heated beverages or soups. Likewise, Xerox is also in danger of becoming generic, as is Kleenex, because people use the trademark to describe the product itself rather than the brand of the product they're describing. This is why some companies insert the word "brand" after the trademark to reinforce that the generic term should not be used, such as "Kleenex brand tissue."

Developers can quickly and effectively build their brand by choosing strong trademarks before registration. Again, intellectual property is merely another framework and in a developer's toolbox. By integrating such tools and tactics into business and product development, a developer not only increases the value of the product but the business itself. In fact, after examining the extremely successful apps in the various app stores, one thing becomes startlingly clear—brand development and subsequent licensing can be a critical element in the success of a product.

LICENSING

Speaking of brand development, while initial sales may be influenced by the quality of an app, it is not the determining factor for continued success. For example, although it would be easy to say that the Angry Birds franchise resulted from a great game that "clicked" with customers, such a suggestion would ignore the tremendous amount of effort by Rovio in building the brand. From inception to the very latest installment, the company developed with an eye toward the brand. The brand became the product and ultimately determined the scope of its own success.

At its core, Angry Birds is merely a physics engine with integrated elements of gameplay. Why then, did it spawn multiple sequels and a motion picture? The answer lies with Rovio seeing beyond the game. Further, without licensing, most of what Rovio has accomplished would have been impossible. There would be no Star Wars branded version of the game. There would be no Angry Birds Rio. And there would definitely be no overabundance of Angry Birds pillows, stickers, plush toys, blankets and other merchandise.

So what is licensing and why is it important? More to the point, how can an indie coder or small firm use licensing as part of an integrated development strategy in the App Era? The first thing to make clear about a license is that, in every transaction, there is a licensor and a licensee. The licensor owns (or has the right to license) a particular intellectual property asset. The licensee wishes to use that technology and, generally, pays a fee for such use.

Although this may sound rudimentary, it is important to mention because the nature of the relationship involves an inherent disparity of power between licensor and licensee. Understanding that imbalance and its effect on negotiating position is what makes the difference between a mutually beneficial licensing setup and disaster.

Generally, it is better to be a licensor than a licensee. A license is usually accompanied by rules and restrictions on what can and cannot be done with the licensed technology. This subordinate position is not preferred because the ultimate decision maker in terms of the licensed asset is the licensor. As such, a licensor can ultimately wield as much power over a developer's business as an unruly partner within the company itself.

To avoid such situations, it is important to evaluate

each license for its relative importance to the project. Before entering into any license, a developer should always ask, "Is this something that could be developed independently?" If an alternative solution can be created in-house within the budget and time constraints of the project, licensing is not the answer. In some cases, however, there may be substantial benefit, especially with regard to development cost or time, to forgo an independently developed solution. Ultimately, this will depend squarely on the developer, the product, the budget and the resources on hand. There is no right answer but, again, if a developer has carefully analyzed their business structure and intellectual property as recommended earlier, the answer will be all that more clear.

If a developer chooses to develop an internal

solution rather than license another product, things change significantly. In such event, the concept of licensing the results, essentially becoming a licensor to those developers that do not have the luxury of time and resources, becomes a potentially lucrative additional revenue stream. For example, a developer may spend the bulk of their budget and resources developing a particular engine or framework, while the primary product is only moderately successful. The engine, however, is an intellectual asset, capable of being licensed (or sold) to others with the same needs. In this way, secondary bits and pieces can become part of the core development strategy.

PATENTS

Patents protect inventions. Unlike copyright and trademark, patent is concerned with the tangible things that an inventor reduces to practice, i.e. things that are actually constructed. As a result, actual creation of the device that will be the subject of the patent is mandatory to seek patent protection. Thus, patents protect ideas but only in the limited sense that those ideas are capable of becoming reality. Without this requirement, as with copyright, patents could issue for mere thoughts, decreasing the storehouse of ideas by locking the best and brightest inside the imagination.

The primary function of the patent system is to promote innovation by awarding an inventor with a monopoly (exclusive right) to make and sell a patented item for a limited time (currently 20 years in the United States), after which the patent expires and the invention is no longer protected. Although a worthy goal, the development of the system has been convoluted and, combined with powerful financial interests, the method of promotion has been defined by financial reward. As a result, patents are seen as hot-ticket, valuable assets on the road to riches, rather than a motivating force to produce something artful. Theoretical arguments aside, it is the financial aspect of the modern patent system that has moved it far beyond the boundaries of common sense and rationality. The system that exists today, in the App Era, is one defined by access and resources, rather than innovation.

To fully prosecute a patent to get a registration takes an enormous amount of money. A full-fledged patent application can cost upwards of

$10,000 or more, depending on the scale and desirability of the patent. Needless to say, most indie and small developers do not have the financial wherewithal to afford such an endeavor, leaving the patent landscape mostly to the larger players. This shift in power is a stark contrast to the days when a solo inventor had a real opportunity to acquire a patent. Yet, the barrier to entry that exists today makes that nearly impossible. This is especially true in technology patents where patent activity is more concentrated than it has ever been.

However, this is not to say that developers should not consider patents a strategic tool in intellectual property planning. It is distinctly possible, depending on the project, that a patentable invention exists and should be protected. This is particularly true in projects that involve hardware which, by its very nature, tends to be an inventive endeavor. In projects lacking a hardware focus, the scope of patentability diminishes significantly, except in the case of software patents, a type of intellectual property that is currently the subject of intense debate.

The software patent, more or less, is based on a process or method of computation in software. The validity of its very existence is tied to the questionable aspect of these types of patents which, at their very core, are nothing more than an idea. Some argue that an algorithm or procedure implementing a particular method satisfies the patent requirement of an invention being reduced to practice. Others claim there is no real invention, only the offshoot of an idea. Arguments aside, the method patent has been embraced in the United States and, unfortunately, looks to be a highly migratory idea in years to come.

An extensive analysis of the software patent debate is beyond the scope of this book. The effects of that debate, however, are particularly applicable to the notion that developers must integrate legal analysis into their development process. Regardless of the arguments against the software patent, it nonetheless exists in the United States, one of the largest marketplaces. Not only do they exist, but very powerful intellectual property management firms have elevated the practice to a business model, effortless in methodology and ruthless in execution. These "businesses" do not produce anything yet sue others that do. Like Gordon Gecko, they create nothing. Rather, they own.

The only effective strategy to combat the powerful

forces aligning behind the patent system is to acknowledge, understand and implement. Simply avoiding the issue altogether is the worst possible choice to make. In the App Era, the simple act of coding can be tantamount to hundreds of millions of dollars of patent infringement liability. It is therefore critical that developers familiarize themselves with what patents are, how they come into being and how to fight them using effective business structuring as discussed above. Such knowledge will empower an App Make to successfully defend against the atrocities of the modern software patent and evaluate their own intellectual property portfolios for potentially patentable assets.

To begin, the required elements of a patent are 1) patentable subject matter, 2) novelty, 3) usefulness and 4) non-obviousness. The first requirement is relatively easy to meet and includes inventions of processes, machines, manufactured articles or compositions of matter. Non-functional descriptive material, such as books, data structures and abstract laws of nature are specifically excluded from material that can be patented.

Note that the above is taken from the United States, a jurisdiction with the broadest statutory list of patentable subject matter in the world. It is included specifically because developers face their greatest challenges from patent trolls in the United States and should be familiar with that particular system. Additionally, most governments worldwide have harmonized, or are in the process of harmonizing, their intellectual property regimes with that of the United States. As the dominant schema, it is by far the most dangerous and the most relevant to our discussion here.

Secondly, patentable inventions must be new in the sense that the article to be patented must not be known to the public, described in a publication or used or offered for sale publicly more than one year before the filing date of the patent application. The novelty requirement is usually determined in terms of the "prior art" that exists surrounding the invention. Simply put, has it ever existed before? Such material can include journal articles, descriptions, actual inventions or even references to the invention anywhere in the world. As you can imagine, then, the prior art research process is one of the most expensive and time consuming parts of the patent application process.

Third, the invention must be useful in that it has a practical purpose and can operate according to that purpose. In other words, the invention must do what it purports to do. This requirement is the most easy to meet of the statutory requirements, since most inventions do serve some purpose and operate with the goal of achieving that purpose. It is fair to say that most inventions meet the standard, especially concerning inventions in technology industry.

Lastly, an invention must not only be new and useful, it must also be "non-obvious" to others trained in the particular field in which the invention is operating. The invention must not simply be an iteration of another such that any individual possessing ordinary skill in the art, or industry, could have developed the same article. Thus, a patentable invention cannot be something that another in the relevant industry would have logically and eventually thought of based on other inventions. In order to meet this requirement, the invention is compared to all existing prior art to determine whether someone else in the field would have made the logical leap and developed the invention in the patent application.

This analysis is difficult, time consuming and, if contested, extremely expensive. Not only must extensive prior art be collected and analyzed, but all aspects of existing inventions must be compared against the invention in the application to see if it is truly non-obvious or merely iterative. Thus, if it exists or has been described anywhere else in the world, it is not novel. Even if the invention is novel, it must be non-obvious and so thoroughly imaginative such that no one else in the field would have developed it. This is an incredibly high standard to meet. However, as the old saying goes, if you throw enough money at a problem, it tends to solve itself.

For indie coders and small firms, though, patents are likely to be more of a reactive problem. With the admittedly high requirements of patentability, software patents demand a highly innovate computational process or method. Determining whether such functions are patentable are beyond the scope of this book, yet it is safe to say that the average app will react to patent law defensively rather than offensively. This is not necessarily a bad thing, since the business of a successful App Making company is just that—making apps. The world is full of trolls and the sickness of greed. If an app has truly patentable elements, they should be protected, but if not, so be it.

Patents will therefore be more of a pain-in-the-ass than intellectual property portfolio building tool.

Patent trolls will most surely assert one of their many purportedly valid patents against a successful app, and even apps with low to moderate revenue production have prompted pre-litigation demand notices. Rest assured, wherever there is money or potential money, trolls are not far behind. Therefore, in regard to patent law, developers must make intellectual property portfolio generation and analysis an important part of their business and product development strategy.

A critical part of such an analysis should include the initial determination of whether a patent application needs to be filed in the first place, even in the event that patentable subject matter exists. This is because the patent application process requires total disclosure of how to create the invention listed in the application. Everything about the article for which the application is being filed must be sufficiently disclosed such that a person of reasonable skill in the art can assemble the device.

While this may seem counterintuitive, the mandate is designed to encourage public disclosure of patentable items in exchange for the rights given to the inventor under the patent. It is an initial substantive check against the inventor's desire for protection against their willingness to release the claimed item to the public. Recall that the principal goal of patent law is to promote innovation which thereby enriches and benefits the public. Therefore, all applications begin with the risk of disclosing a potentially profitable item to the public in exchange for the protection of being the only source for it.

Obviously, the disclosure requirement involves a certain amount of risk. In publishing instructions on how to build the patent, an inventor enables the public to create knock-offs or gain insight into the patent's usefulness. Thus, some companies and inventors purposefully choose not to apply after carefully weighing the benefits of protection for a limited time against the risk in competitive advantage presented by disclosure. The decision is a complex one and involves a variety of factors but the point is that certain intellectual assets can be so valuable over the life of a company such that a limited patent term is insufficient protection. In those cases, the device or method is better left as a trade secret, which will be discussed below.

In the App Era, even the simplest programatic idea can become the subject of a patent troll's claim against a coder's business. A deep and thorough understanding of an app's intellectual property is the only method by which victory is possible against trolls seeking to extort their "share" of a developer's revenue. By knowing and understanding the potential claims against the code in an app, a developer can either use alternative code or methods. At the very least, an educated decision may be made concerning the scope of an app's release, choosing to avoid jurisdictions in which the app may be subject to claims by trolls.

Thoughtful analysis of a company's intellectual property portfolio and knowledge of what may be asserted against the intellectual property contained in an app highlights how different areas of law overlap to address issues. If, for instance, it is learned that a particular patent troll in the United States has a good claim against a particular method or aspect of an app, a suitably resistant business structure can be implemented to shield the company. A multi-tiered structure in which a holding company owns the intellectual property with a licensee entity in the United States can sometimes insulate against otherwise potentially massive damages.

This is the ultimate intersection of code and law, by which a developer uses one system in furtherance of another. The law shifts from being an expensive hindrance to a battle chest containing strategies and tactics that assist in the overall mission of making great stuff. Moreover, when the app ships, it does so with a well-constructed structure and solid intellectual property portfolio, fully prepared to battle the App Era. This cooperative fusion defines a truly well-executed app.

THE PARTS BIN

There are some forms of intellectual property that are not registered with a governmental authority. Such non-statutory (meaning it exists irrespective of there being no law governing it) intellectual property is generally protected under legal doctrines that have developed over time through case decisions. As such, this type of intellectual property is the least valuable in terms of building an intellectual property portfolio There is no certain damage award set by statute, no presumption of validity (because there is no registration) and no legal foundation for licensing revenue. Still, non-statutory intellectual is valuable and, in some cases, even more valuable than statutory intellectual property if confidentiality is maintained.

One of the most common types of non-statutory intellectual property is the trade secret. A trade secret is simply a secret that gives a company a competitive advantage. Trade secrets can be, and often are, technical in nature, such as how to assemble a particular product or a particular method or process that is either incapable of being patented or something the company does not desire to disclose in a patent application. Trade secrets can also include proprietary means of production, components, recipes, formulas or methods of assembly. Interestingly, many of the most valuable trade secrets are intellectual assets that were purposefully not patented.

The formula for Coca-Cola, for example, has never been registered as a patent. If it had been, the Coca-Cola Company would have lost the exclusive right to the formula after the patent expired.

Additionally, because patent applications require total disclosure of the item in the patent application, it is likely that it would have been copied, diluted, mutated or otherwise misappropriated shortly after the application was filed. To prevent such detrimental effects to one of the world's most valuable intellectual assets, the Coca-Cola formula has remained a trade secret. It is not patented or otherwise registered with any governing body. Only a handful of individuals within the Coca-Cola Company know the formula and extreme care is taken to prevent unauthorized disclosure or theft.

The example of Coca-Cola highlights the distinguishing characteristic of a trade secret as something that is valuable and gives a company a competitive advantage. Additionally, to remain a trade secret, a company must actively protect and maintain it as a secret. The Coca-Cola Company has an army of attorneys and investigators whose purpose is to protect the formula from being released to the public. Such high-profile efforts are not required, however. There must merely be some active participation by the company in protecting the trade secret and maintaining its secrecy.

Trade secrets are not officially recognized by statute as a form of intellectual property. However, as can be seen in the Coca-Cola example, trade secrets can nonetheless be powerful and valuable assets. They are protected primarily by common law rights, based on previous cases decided by courts, and the law of contract. When dealing with a trade secret, a company will use confidentiality and non-disclosure agreements, often buried in an employment agreement, for those employees that come in contact or deal with the trade secret.

These types of agreements are generally enforceable, especially concerning trade secrets that for the core or basis of a particular product, such as the formula for Coca-Cola.

When applied to apps, trade secrets can comprise a valuable portion of the intellectual property involved. For example, there may be an exclusive system of computation, a highly defined method or process of selection or a proprietary algorithm contained in the code that gives a similar competitive advantage. As such, the trade secret should be identified and properly protected through clear and effective contracts with employees, contractors or agents and internal processes designed to maximize security and promote secrecy. If these steps are followed, and especially given the unruly nature of software patents, a developer may choose to selectively enforce trade secret protection rather than attempt a patent application, even if the item would otherwise qualify as patentable.

A second category of non-statutory intellectual property is confidential information, which is broadly defined as an any information which gives a company a business advantage. As with trade secrets, confidential information is protection by common law legal theories and contract. As such, it carries the same risk that, once disclosed, the information ceases to give a competitive advantage to the company. Confidential information may form the basis of a particular trade secret and vice versa. As such, there is a general category of confidential information that perhaps does not rise to level of a trade secret, such as customer lists, contact information, price sheets or terms of sale. Although such information may also be a trade secret, it is usually referred to as confidential information.

Generally, confidential information will be specifically addressed in either a non-disclosure agreement or as part of an employment agreement. Such agreements usually state that, in consideration for employment or work on a particular project, they will be given access to particular information that in not known outside the company. These agreements are generally held valid and severe consequences can result from disclosing confidential information in an unauthorized manner. These agreements are particularly useful for solo and indie developers, as they provide good protection for intellectual assets that are deemed too secretive to patent or otherwise incapable of being registered.

While there are other forms of non-statutory intellectual property, such as trade dress (a particular style or look that is not trademarked), they are not as particularly relevant to developers as are trade secrets and confidential information. If protected correctly and consistently, these types of assets can become an integral part of a developer's development process. The key, however, is that such materials remain protected and secret.

Thus, the first tension for in a developer's growth cycle will be the hiring of employees or contractors. In certain cases, especially in the App Era context, disclosure is necessary to the development goals of the project. As such, any disclosure should be handled with extreme caution after ensuring that all contracts, be they with employees, contractors, investors or suppliers contain sufficiently powerful non-disclosure provisions. Remember, the only method of protecting non-statutory intellectual property is via common law, the application of which generally requires a lawsuit to be filed, and by contract.

Because of this, the scope of proaction afforded to assets otherwise unprotected by statutory systems such as copyright, trademark and patent should be as broad and uniform as possible. We will discuss the specifics of the contractual provisions below but, for purposes of this chapter developers should realize that not all valuable intellectual property will be subject to governmental registration. In some cases, such as with potentially patentable items, such registration may not even be desirable. Regardless, unregistered assets are still protected, albeit by different mechanisms.

SUMMARY

Apps are more than mere bundles of code and resources. Apps are bundles of those things plus valuable legal rights that include a variety of intellectual assets. These assets can include copyrights, trademarks, license rights, patents (or potential patents), trade secrets and confidential information. If viewed as an integral part of the product development process, intellectual property can become the cornerstone of a company's overall worth. Intellectual property should be considered as essential as the code in which it takes shape, a wrapper that provides protection, security and value.

Intellectual property rights accrue to a creator from the moment of creation and continue to grown in business and legal benefit. Copyright, for example, exists the second that expression is fixed in a tangible media. There are certain benefits of registering that copyright, such as presumed validity and statutory damages, but the ownership manifests when it is created. For example, when a developer codes an app, a copyright interest is created with the first line of code written. Thereafter, the developer is the exclusive holder of the right to legally reproduce, prepare derivative works of, distribute, perform and display the work.

The same is true of trademarks, which are words, symbols graphics or phrases that designate the origin (source company) of a product. These things are protected trademarks from the moment first used in commerce. As with copyright, there are benefits to registering the trademark, most notably the presumption of validity that accompanies a registration. By submitting the trademark for registration and completing the application process, the trademark is "proved up" and must be shown to be invalid to be challenged. Trademarks can become an incredibly valuable intellectual asset for a company through consistent branding efforts.

License rights are also part of a well-planned intellectual property portfolio. A license is a contractual right given from the owner of an intellectual asset to another party that grants certain rights to use, sell, distribute or develop the asset. Developers can use both inbound and outbound licensing in very productive ways. An inbound license can be used to integrate a particular framework or product into a developer's app, avoiding the cost and resources of developing the desired feature. Likewise, if a developer has developed something that would be useful for others, an outbound license for the use of the asset creates an additional, and potentially very valuable, revenue stream for the company.

Patents may also prove valuable to a developer, as protection for novel inventions. However, due to the current debate surrounding software patents, it is likely that most solo and indie developers will be reacting to patents rather than seeking their registration. While it is certainly possible for a developer to create a method of computation or algorithm so unique and novel in its design to be worthy of patent protection, the average app is unlikely to include such elements.

The downside to this is that patent trolls have amassed large, sweeping portfolios of patents that purport to cover most existing processes. a developer will be dealing with patent law issues even if patent protection is not a consideration in the development process. Therefore, it is crucial to understand patent issue and analyze product development with a perspective that identifies problems before they develop.

Finally, there are some intellectual assets that have no formal registration scheme or statute that specifically protects them. These types of asset, of which trade secrets and confidential information are most relevant to developers, are protected through case law decisions by courts and contract law. To adequately safeguard these assets, which can sometimes be more valuable to a company than a patent or registered asset, proper care must be taken to maintain secrecy and confidentiality.

Such precautions require through planning and

well-drafted contracts within all elements of the company, from employees and contractors to negotiations. Additionally, systems must be implemented to shield trade secrets and confidential information from public disclosure which, if it occurs, renders the value of the asset worthless.

CONTRACTS

THE DEVIL'S TONGUE

If a developer's business structure is the house where assets and intellectual property live, contracts are the doors and locks. These agreements bolt the entrances and exits of a company and provide a mechanism by which information, goods, services and people flow. Without contracts, legal and business actions exist in a vacuum with no grounds for legitimacy. Further, written agreements serve a fundamental purpose at the intersection of code and law—defining expectations.

There are a great variety of contracts that govern different types of activities. For example, when a formal business structure is created, a formation document is created to describe who owns the company and their relative responsibilities, duties, privileges and rights. These types of contracts, such as a shareholder agreement in a corporation or an operating agreement in a limited liability company, are essential agreements between the company and owners of shares.

Similarly, there are a vast array of corporate agreements necessary to buy or sell shares and transfer ownership of certain assets, such as intellectual property created by the founders. Of course, anything involving money is heavily documented, from lending and forbearance agreements to the payment of additional capital contributions to the company. Additionally, the company may execute agreements for the issuance of stock options and other financial awards. All of these things are largely participatory activities that contracts seek to either enable or disable, depending on the circumstance.

Authorizing actions and defining rights, responsibilities and roles are the ways in which agreements set and maintain the expectations of the parties. In this way, everyone involved knows precisely what is expected of them, what rights may be exercised and when actions may be taken. For developers, a contract can be thought of as an API (Application Programming Interface), interaction schemas which enable enhanced functionality, speed access or increase efficiency.

A written agreement is the command console to which the company may turn for operating instructions and, most importantly, the value that will be returned for a given action. Accordingly, each API/agreement will have its own unique set of conditions, qualifiers and rules governing performance, timing, and scope of action. However, there are several things that all contracts, as promises that each party make to one another, have in common and require.

First, there must be offer and acceptance to properly form any type of contractual relationship. In other words, one party cannot merely decide that a contract exists then attempt to enforce it. The proof of a contract's existence rests with the making of an offer and a resulting acceptance of that offer. While the subtleties of the offer and acceptance requirement are best debated in law school classrooms, the point can be efficiently illustrated with a simple example. If someone wishes to purchase a car, they will generally begin the process by asking how much it costs. Once a sales price has been stated, it is considered the offer for a contract of sale. The buyer can either accept the offer or reject it and present a counteroffer, which must then be accepted by the seller.

As you can see, there is a great potential complexity in the offer and acceptance phase of a contract. For our purposes here, developers should be aware that without a stated offer and an acceptance of that offer, there simply is no contract. This can be extremely important in hiring contractors and negotiating licenses or other contracts for sale. A great deal of misunderstandings and disagreements in contractual disputes can be traced to confusion or misinterpretations in offer and acceptance, leading to a raft of issues in later negotiations when the agreement is put into writing.

Being in writing is generally a good idea with most

contracts, although there are specific types that must be in writing to be valid. Governed by an old, dusty and equally important legal doctrine called the Statute of Frauds (which is usually codified by statute in most jurisdictions), contracts for the sale of land, sales over a certain amount and other specific agreements must be contained in a writing in order to be enforceable. Although not directly relevant for our purposes, it is worth noting that all transfers or assignments of intellectual must be in writing. Otherwise, any such transfer may as well not even exist, except perhaps in theory.

Contracts for services, such as contractor and employment agreements, are not generally required to be in writing. Underscoring a general legal principle rooted in good, old-fashioned common sense, however, contracts for services should always be in writing. In fact, developers should ensure that all contracts executed in pursuit of their business, and other aspects of their lives for that matter, are in writing and treated with reverence. Although this may seem overly formal, there is absolutely nothing more distracting to the business of making apps than a resource intensive search for evidence that proves and enforces an oral agreement. Simply putting agreements in writing can rescue a developer from a litany of issues and problems.

Developers should, as we have discussed in the context of different legal issues, know their business inside and out. There is simply no substitute for a written agreement governing freelance and employee relationships, licensing, sales, transfers and other day-to-day operational issues rife with potential for uproarious attacks and inconvenient setbacks. Putting things in writing, despite how simple they seem or the long standing relationships of those involved, forces order on the chaos. Written agreements strip away the obfuscations of emotion and inflection and clarify, sometimes in exceptionally striking fashion, what has been agreed to and what has not. At their simplest and best, contracts solve disputes by their very existence and obviate the emotionally intensive and resource draining process of figuring out just what the hell went wrong.

In many cases, the thing that goes wrong directly relates to what each party receives from the other under the terms of the contract. These disputes underscore the value of a writing and illustrate a "bargained for exchange," a contractual validity requirement where each party gets something for its performance. The "something" is referred to in legal terms as consideration and can include money, services or property that a person gives to another to prompt the performance of the other under the terms of the contract.

For example, if a developer wants to license a particular framework from a larger firm, there will usually be a license agreement stating that the developer may use the framework in exchange for certain compensation. Legally, the developer receives the license as a result or "in consideration" of the fee. In this case, the consideration for the existence of the contract is a fixed sum of money, whatever the number, and the license is given in exchange for that bargained for amount changing hands.

Contracts must have some kind of consideration or there is no palpable agreement between the parties, rendering the contract invalid. While there is no strict requirement on what consideration must be given in a particular agreement, there has to be at least something exchanged for the mutual promises made. Examples include money, doing something, not doing something, giving up certain rights, receiving employment or exclusivity of one type or another. Thus, regardless of how it is manifested, consideration must exist at the time of contract formation.

There are some instances in which even the stated consideration will be judged regarding its sufficiency for producing a legally binding contract. This is why the law requires the exchange of consideration by each party to be "bargained for" by the other. Whatever is given to secure the mutual contractual promise must be "won" in the sense that it results from negotiating or compromise through discussions. Therefore, the thing given by one party to another in a contract must be something that has been worked for and sought after by the other.

As a result, consideration is something legally desirable, rather than an action that would be done even if the contract did not exist or at the total discretion of the party pledging it. For instance, a party cannot do something "if it wants to" because nothing is given to secure the mutual promise of the other. In other words, both parties to a contract have to pledge something that the other wants and tender it as part of the contract's formation and inception.

For developers, consideration will usually be either money or services. A freelance developer, for instance, may provide coding hours to acquire an equity position in a newly formed developer.

Conversely, a developer may compensate its development staff with shares of stock rather than cash. Conversely, a well funded developer may pay its contract developers a fixed hourly amount. Likewise, a a useful framework or component may be licensed for inclusion in another product in exchange for a stake in the resulting sales. Be it money or services, developers should always not what the consideration for a given agreement is and how it is to be given. Doing so ensures a fair, beneficial contract for all parties.

Although there are additional legal requirements concerning contract formation, such as intent of the parties, age of consent and other largely fact dependent issues, developers are most directly affected by the three discussed in this chapter. Again, with awareness and knowledge comes power. By being aware of the ways in which contracts affect their business, developers will not only become more well equipped to handle business arrangements but be able to negotiate strong, secure agreements that prevent future disputes. With that in mind, we will now discuss specific contracts, their structure and how they are useful to developers.

EMPLOYMENT & CONSULTING AGREEMENTS

Employment and consulting (or contractor) agreements are a fundamental aspect of a developer's contractual relationships. Most growth related companies either have more than one active developer or a team of programmers working on different aspects of a particular project. Still, even in indie coder shops, the legal relationship between the business structure and the developer as an individual is governed by an employment or contractor agreement. In such instances, the relationship largely relates to the transfer of intellectual property from developer to company as it is created. This is beneficial for many reasons, some of which we have already discussed. In other cases where there are multiple coders, the existence of formalized employment and contractor relationships, and the legal implications of each, are of utmost importance.

At the onset, developers should note that employees carry with them a great deal of legal liability, far more so than independent contractors. There are a great number of factors that determine whether someone working for a company is truly an employee or a contractor, even despite what their contract states. Generally, the more control a company has over an individual will be determinative of whether that individual is legally categorized as an employee or contractor. For instance, if a company executes a contractor agreement with a coder, then provides office space, materials, computers and resources, along with orders and timelines and direction, that individual is likely an employee. Such missteps in categorization do not necessarily impose contractual liability but could expose the company to governmental sanctions, fines or severe penalties.

To avoid these types of issues, employment and contractor agreements must work in tandem with how the individual is treated and all aspects of the contract must be strictly enforced. An example of the possible negative consequences that could result from non-enforcement is when a contractor suddenly begins acting like an employee and is treated as such by the company, despite the contractor agreement. Recall that companies are generally more liable for employees versus contractors. In the above example, a contractor that is tacitly acknowledged as an employee creates huge potential liability for negligence, wrongful acts or omissions. Thus, it is critical that developers firmly establish whether a staff member is an employee or contractor and steadfastly adhere to the terms of the resulting agreement.

With such a contract, the financial result will largely be the same in that the company receives programming and the coder receives some form of compensation. Beyond the practical effect, however, contractors will generally require a greater degree of contractual security privacy enforcement, such as non-disclosure and non-compete clauses. Also crucial to implement and enforce is a validly constructed transfer and assignment of intellectual property rights. This is especially key in the context of App Making sense because contractors, by their very nature, are potential competitors. As such, anything they can create must be properly labeled as a work for hire such that the rights are assigned to the company paying for their services, with a fallback assignment and transfer of rights executed at the various deliverable dates.

Employees, on the other hand, create intellectual property as a direct result, and in consideration of, the employment relationship. As a result, anything an employee creates belongs to the company automatically, with no assignment or transfer transaction necessary. Still, it is always a good idea to recite such terms of the relationship in the employment contract to avoid confusion and, most importantly, future disputes. Remember, contracts should solve problems merely by existing so anything that clarifies and underscores the intent of the parties and the overall legal status and effect of their relationship promotes success.

Something that should definitely be addressed in

an employment or contractor agreement, in conjunction with clarifying intellectual property ownership as discussed above, is the issue of access. By design, product development requires a great deal of access to a developer's intellectual property. As a result, every contractor and employee is a potential leak of a developer's confidential information and trade secrets. Therefore, all agreements, no matter how small the work, should contain confidentiality and non-disclosure provisions with clearly defined rules governing what materials are covered by the restrictions.

Generally, most agreements tend to lock down anything and everything disclosed to the employee or contractor. This is much more important in the context of freelancers, which typically use their own resources, such as phones and computers. With employees, it is much easier to enforce confidentiality provisions and restrict access to certain materials by using company resources as gatekeepers. Additionally, recovery of information shared with employees is easily accomplished by retrieval of the equipment assigned to them. Contractors, on the other hand, are free to roam as lone warriors of the apocalypse, the coding equivalent to rōnin samurai. There is no general provision entitling a contracting party to inspect or otherwise commandeer a contractor's equipment without litigation.

From that perspective, it is easy to see how developers benefit from keeping freelance coders on the shortest of leashes. Apart from physical and operational restrictions of access, the contractor agreement used to secure the coder's services should, in every conceivable way, lock down any shared materials or confidential information that changes hands. Remember, the goal is to draft away potential problems before they arise. By defining precise expectations in secrecy and non-disclosure, along with penalties for any breach, contractors are less likely to misappropriate or disclose shared information.

Another key aspect of employment agreements in particular is the non-solicitation agreement. This is a promise on the part of the prospective employee that, in consideration of the job received, they will not actively solicit or "hire away" any other employees of a company if they leave their position and start a competing business. This is important on many different levels, not the least of which is to prevent "brain drain" within organizations such as technology developers where the talent pool is often as valuable a resource as the die or initial technologies being developed. Indeed, some developers are acquired by larger companies solely to capture the existing employees, as the cumulative performance and team metrics may surpass even that of the technology being developed within the company. For developers, this is a viable basis to lock down the existing employment roster by preventing talented individuals from being lured away by someone who leaves the company. However, there is an even more significant reason to prevent such an occurrence.

The siphoning of talented, creative minds is cause for serious concern yet the loss of a large portion of such resources can be disastrous to a developer's intellectual property portfolio. Within technology companies, employees often handle the core of the relevant assets that comprise the value of the company's products. If a significant portion of those employees leave en masse, so does the building and development impetus for those assets and a sizable chunk of the knowledge related to getting things done. Additionally, in such instances, confidential information gushes from the wound with such speed and volume that the damage is nearly impossible to correct. Employees, armed with everything they know about a company's products, customer lists, pricing information, forecasts, sales figures, business plans and strategy are much too valuable a resource to lose, especially to a solicitor.

This is why anti-solicitation provisions in employment agreements are incredibly important. In most cases, they can prove more beneficial than the confidentiality and non-disclosure provisions, simply because the accumulated value of an employee is so much more than secrets and plans. The total gain to a company from a well-integrated and fully functioning team is simply immeasurable. Therefore, "protecting the herd" from poaching is tantamount to building a fortress around the company itself. Additionally, there are more complex mechanisms available to protect the company from employees that would otherwise seek to do harm to their former employer.

The non-compete agreement is a tool by which a developer can effectively force a former employee to work outside the sphere of influence and control enjoyed during the term of their employment. The provision essentially locks the employee into a term during which they are completely unable to use the confidential information and skills they have acquired at their former company. Although the specific provisions and effective length of the non-compete term varies, the agreements are generally held valid, as long as the limitations are reasonable.

As a result, courts usually require some manner of limitation on a non-compete agreement's restrictiveness to enforce them. Judges are quite hesitant to impose broad, sweeping limitations on an individual's ability to practice within their field, particularly in an economic downturn. The resulting tension between an employer's right to control the performance potential in which they invested and an individual's right to work is a deeply complex issue beyond the scope of this book. However, if adequately limited and reasonable in scope and application, non-compete provisions give a developer time to make use of resources developed by the former employee and a strategy to handle the loss of key staff.

WARRANTIES & INDEMNIFICATION

Besides mutual promises between the signing parties, most contracts contain a series of warranties. These are related to the typical product warranty that accompanies consumer goods but concern the authority of the parties to act or the goods or services that are produced by the contractual performance. There are a variety of warranty types that are either specifically included or excluded, such as whether the parties have authority to act in the contract or on behalf of the business entity for whom they are signing. However, for purposes of our discussion, most developers should be concerned with warranties relating to intellectual property ownership and rights of third parties in freelance agreements, as well as standards and security compliance.

It is vital for developers using independent contractors to ensure deliverable code does not infringe third-party rights. In freelance contracts, this is normally addressed by requiring the coder to provide a warranty that all deliverables will be provided free from any encumbrances or third-party claims. Also included in the warranty will be an express acknowledgment that the contractor is working from a code base that does not infringe the rights of any third-party. This is hugely important because third-party code being wrapped into a project may result in massive liability for a developer. All freelancers working on a project should be made aware of this provision at the time of signing, especially if they are not represented by an attorney.

Putting contract coders on high alert that they are ultimately responsible for infringing materials included in their deliverables is an excellent way to prevent infringement claims before they are made. Otherwise, the mindset becomes significantly more lax regarding ownership of included frameworks or pieces of code. Further still, some freelancers are completely unaware of infringement or infringement issues at the onset, so including the provision and actively discussing its effect will increase not only the security of developers code but contribute to a freelancer's best practices. Often, the simple expectation that a contractor is aware of these issues is enough to move awareness levels forward and increase the efficacy of the delivered product.

Still, what good is a contractual provision if it effectively has no teeth for enforcement? Warranty provisions result in the conscious undertaking of responsibility if the expectation of providing code free from claims is not met. The resulting responsibility, or duty, is expressed by another contractual provision known as the indemnity clause. This simple statement, which can be as short as a sentence or two in simple agreements, provides that the person providing a warranty for claim-free code will pay for any claims that result for its use. In other words, if a contractor makes the mistake of including elements that are subject to ownership claims by third parties, that contractor must pay for any damages or any costs resulting from the infringing materials.

Indemnification is an often misunderstood and feared legal mechanism. For a developer in the App Era, however, this simple little provision may be all that stands between the company and litigation. It is important to note, however, that indemnification is only as good as the ability of the party promising indemnity to pay it. That is to say, a developer cannot get blood from a stone and, if a freelance coder has no resources to indemnify a developer, there is simply nothing to get. This is why it is beneficial to work with those contract coders that are well established or have adequate business insurance. Again, it cannot be stressed enough that awareness of the legal topics in this book increase awareness of a developer's business and, therefore, add value and protection to all assets of the business.

For example, armed with a basic knowledge of warranties and indemnification, a developer can choose only reputable freelancers or those capable of withstanding third-party infringement indemnification claims. Conversely, such knowledge enables a developer to only contract out non-critical portions of a project.

Fundamentally, a working understanding how contracts affect a business and its products is the best and least expensive method of avoiding infringement claims before they arise. Proper selection of contractors using clearly defined criteria such as those listed above can prove invaluable to the growth and protection of a developer's intellectual property portfolio.

Similarly, developers should ensure that contract developers provide warranties relating to adherence to industry standards and security protocols. These types of provisions are becoming increasingly important in the App Era, mostly due to social apps and tools that have access to user's personal identifying information. Although it is likely that contract coders will not work directly with any customer data, it is possible, especially in circumstances requiring live testing or access to a developer's internal network. Apart from the obvious matter of protecting the company's resources and intellectual property, the ancillary liability that could result from a breach of private customer data or location information is potentially very large.

As a result, freelancers should provide a warranty that any work performed will adhere to reasonable security and data protection standards. This is even more critical if the app is being developed for private use rather than a wide-scale consumer release. For example, if a developer is developing a piece of software that deals with business to business location information, all work performed should be performed strictly within certain standards. While this is true of work performed internally by employees, it is even more important with freelancers who, because no employer-employee relationship exits, are technically third parties as far as the resulting app is concerned. Freelancers do not legally answer to the company and are therefore as unpredictable as the weather. This underscores the principal message of this section: all third-party development must be as contractually secure as possible.

ARBITRATION & MEDIATION

In any contract, a developer may specify that any disputes arising out of or relating to the agreement will be funneled through an informal conflict resolution process called arbitration or mediation. Such a process does not involve a court or a judge, unless a judge is needed to order the process to take place (if, for example, a plaintiff sues without realizing they must arbitrate first). This simple and direct provision can save a developer countless hours of frustration and stress by simply taking litigation out of the equation altogether (see the Litigation and Disputes section below for a discussion of why this is a very good thing).

Secondarily, arbitration provides for a method of choosing the third-party arbitrator. This is a hugely important for developers, since most judges are horribly ill equipped to handle cases involving software, technology or patents. By providing for the selection of an arbitrator with pre-defined technical qualifications, the developer ensures that any disputes arising out of the contract are at least judged in a technically proficient manner. This is not always the case in a court of law and, sometimes, the very opposite. Anything that can be done to ensure an intellectual property or software related issue is being mediated by someone with knowledge of the industry is a very good thing.

Moreover, arbitration can be made binding against the participants, meaning that any decision made will not be appealable in a court of law. Obviously, this has potential negative connotations if a developer breaches one of the terms. However, those developers reading this book are more likely to know the contract's terms and, most importantly, understand the impact of those terms before they are required to perform. Thus, it is more likely than not that a developer will be perform its contractual relations. On that level, a developer has nothing to fear from binding arbitration. Then again, if there is any uncertainty to performance under a particular contract, this element of the provision should be scrutinized.

Also important is the fact that arbitration proceedings are generally confidential. Although there are certain jurisdictions where the provision must specifically state the proceedings will be confidential, there is at least some way to lock down the contents of the dispute resolution process. This is not the case with litigation, where there may be a public record of proceedings. This is less important in cases that involve simple business disputes but, in matters dealing with intellectual property claims, it is essential to maintain confidentiality of the process.

Beyond these considerations, arbitration is much less expensive and time consuming than litigation. This is even more true when an arbitrator with knowledge of the technology industry, software and intellectual property is chosen. These two factors alone, speed and money, should be enough to persuade developers to include arbitration and mediation provisions in all of their contractual agreements. This is an excellent example of how the law can be used an integrated part of the development process. In every contractual engagement, the simple inclusion of these provisions strengthens a developer's business foundation by reallocating resources that would be used for dispute resolution to product development and ongoing operations.

Lastly, there is a certain degree of control that comes from implementing an arbitration provision. It allows a developer to determine, at least in part, every dispute in their contractual sphere. In litigation, the outcome of a dispute is much less certain and prone to variables such as the behavior of the jury, the collective experience and disposition of the judge and the demeanor of the plaintiff and defendant. With arbitration, those elements of the equation are removed. There is no jury to run amok and no judge to inject their own bias. Most importantly, it is much more difficult for the participants to introduce characteristics that would flavor or influence the outcome.

LICENSE AGREEMENTS

We have already discussed how important the licensing of software can be for a developer's business model. If core technologies can be used by other developers working toward the same goal, such products can be used to create additional revenue streams, of which every developer is usually in need. However, there are additional licensing perspectives that developers must consider, including that of the inbound license and end-user license agreements directed toward users of the software.

An inbound license is software or other technologies that flow into a company by way of a license agreement. In this instance, the developer is the licensee, rather than the licensor, and will be the party subject to rules and restrictions on how the licensed property can and cannot be used. This arrangement, as we have briefly discussed before, is a vital part of software development. In some instances, developing an internal solution may prove time consuming or incredibly expensive. Likewise, if there are existing graphical elements, music or audiovisual materials that can be incorporated into an app by way of licensing, the money and effort that would otherwise have been expended on those resources is saved for other aspects of the project.

Licensing is, therefore, both a content acquisition vehicle and resource allocation tool. Again, in allaying a particular project or a company's overall asset portfolio, a developer is at their best and most efficient when they make informed, knowledgeable decisions. Researching which particular resources should be developed versus acquired by license is an indispensable part of that equation. Although it is frequently suggested that developers should "eat their own dog food," licensing can obviate the expenditure of vast amounts of development time. Of course, money is often the guiding factor in this analysis with most developers firmly convinced that it will ultimately be cheaper to develop in-house than acquire technologies through licensing and paying the associated license fee for the asset.

While every circumstance is different, this is usually not the case, especially when looking at developers. Although it seems contrary to logic, in-house development is often not the best choice, especially concerning game or physics engines and graphical, music or audiovisual content. The sheer magnitude of developing those materials can overwhelm most developers and, ultimately, any money saved results in an inferior product.

Secondarily, launch delays of products are directly proportional to the number of technologies developed in-house. In the App Era, the loss of market acquisition time can be critical, especially in certain market segments, such as gaming and social apps. Decisions concerning developing a custom solution or elements versus licensing needs to be thoroughly weighed against the potential loss of time on market and real cost of development.

Inbound licenses will contain many of the provisions discussed in this section and will most certainly touch on or have an impact on other topics covered in this book. Depending on the circumstances, licensing can be one of the most complex and formidable aspects of a developer's business. Legal issues such as term and termination and sub-licensing are quite often the most contested legal issues. Additionally, there are a myriad of business issues such as royalty, payment and branding that need to be proposed, discussed, negotiated and clarified. This is a daunting task but significantly less challenging if a developer follows the strategies outlined here.

The most important thing when reviewing inbound licenses is the specific language of what is being licensed. Although it sounds rather simplistic, the license must specify, at a minimum, the exact property that is being licensed to the developer, the territory for which it is being licensed, whether the use is commercial or noncommercial, what labeling must accompany the use and which additional rights, if any, the developer has to the licensed asset.

For example, if a developer desires to incorporate the licensed property into multiple products, that use must be specifically included in the license. Acquiring the technology for limited use means just what it says—the use is limited to the specific language of the agreement. Any authorized use of a licensed asset must be specifically listed in the agreement.

Although the terms of inbound licenses are highly dependent on the licensor from whom the asset is being acquired, developers are free to dictate the terms of their end-user license agreement. Commonly referred to as the EULA, the end-user license agreement is a private contract between a developer and their customers. This is an excellent example of an outbound license, with the developer as licensor and the resulting end user the licensee.

Viewed by consumers and the mainstream media as burdensome, onerous and heavily complex, EULAs are an important element of a developer's contractual arsenal, completely defining the relationship with a user. Accordingly, EULAs should be viewed as one of the most important contracts a developer will draft and a vital part of development.

There are a variety of important considerations in drafting a well-constructed EULA. For developers, one of the most immediately relevant provisions is the disclaimer of liability. Every app will have a measurable potential liability, just as a rock on an angled mountainside has a certain amount of potential energy. Some apps, however, have far more potential liability than others, such as those that deal with a user's personal information, location or sensitive data.

Developers should generally be concerned with the events for which they disclaim liability but those doing business in the areas listed above should be extra cautious. If sensitive data is being handled, the user should be required to consent and, more specifically, exempt the developer from any resulting liability from the use. More specifically, developers should always comply with any applicable privacy and data processing laws.

A particularly easy to understand example would be an app that collects location information or travel routes, for whatever reason, and uses that data for some specific purpose. If the security of the data is compromised and the information used for some nefarious purpose, the developer would be liable for such use unless the user specifically consents. In other words, if a developer is handling sensitive information, the user must consent to that use and be reasonably informed about what actions will result from the information being used and how they may be affected.

Recall that contracts are the sole means of entry to and exit from the developer's "house" of business. If a visitor may be harmed by entering, they should be alerted to the possibility and consciously accept the risk before they enter. A developer's EULA is the sign posted on the front door advising all those that may enter of what to expect inside. Whatever happens after the user crosses the threshold needs to be disclosed so that the visitor can properly consent to the occurrence of those events.

Legally, of course, criminal acts can never be the valid subject of a contract, so a developer cannot ask a user to consent to willful and intentional criminal uses of their information. However, liability for non-criminal uses of sensitive information, as long as the user is informed and consents, can be properly disclaimed by a developer in a well-constructed EULA. The heart of this issue is whether the user has given their informed consent. And it is user consent that should guide all developers when collecting personal or sensitive information, in addition to complying with privacy laws, of course.

Unlike other legal definitions, which usually require quite a bit of interpretation to fully understand, this one means exactly what it says. If a user is properly informed about what an app will do and the results of the processes and actions that take place such that they are able to knowingly and consciously consent, there is no resulting liability for the developer. This is the primary reason that EULAs should be explicit regarding what an app does, how it works, what data is being collected and what will be done with it once it is disclosed. This is even more true in the App Era where apps are increasingly location and context aware or capable of automatically submitting or retrieving data from an always-on network connection.

As a result, the historical question of whether a developer should develop a privacy policy has been rendered moot. EULAs should always address privacy issues, especially in the context of what personal data is being collected and how it will be used. The disclosure should be as detailed and lengthy as necessary to fully inform the user of what will happen to their data in using the app. This is particularly important in instances where the app is transmitting user generated content, including text, photos and videos to an underlying web or backend service.

In such a case, the user should consent to the transmission and collection, even if the action is voluntary on their part, as with status updates, blog posts or photo sharing. Although some of these shared services will likely rely on API calls to third parties, such as Twitter or Instagram, and will be covered under the EULA for the respective third-party service, a developer should still address any sharing of user content beyond the physical device.

In the event the action is sent to a web or backend

service provided by the developer, there should be a separate EULA, complete with terms that define the use and operation of the service itself. This EULA will govern the user's interaction with the processing of the content as it is received by the app transmitting it. The result is a tiered licensing structure where each activity involving the developer and user are managed by a set of terms and conditions. Such an environment serves two important purposes: 1) the user is alerted to the possible results of their action, both within the app and any post-app processing; and 2) the user, because they use the app and any accompanying services, consents and limits the developer's liability.

Developers often wonder if any of these issues are covered in their relationship with a platform provider as the distribution provider for their apps.

Recall from earlier that providers such as Apple and Google occupy an extremely powerful position in the App Era. They are the sole point of contact for users to learn about and purchase a developer's products. As such, developers often incorrectly assume that the relationship is a mutually beneficial one.

This is very far from the practical application of the platform provider distribution model, as the developer still shoulders virtually all the risk for the operation of their app on a user's device. Even though platform providers provide a "catchall" EULA for purchases made in their respective app store, developers should not rely on it for adequate protection. In short, developers should always have a EULA customized for each of their various apps.

For example, Apple's default agreement merely covers the fundamental contractual relationship and basic elements of intellectual property, consent and limitations. These defaults, however, are insufficient to adequately cover the wide array of apps available. Functions involving user generated content and resulting transmission are not covered, nor is collection or use of personal or location-based information. Worse yet, there are no strict financial limits to a developer's liability in such scenarios. Likewise, third-party content use and warranties are not adequately addressed.

These examples, and several other inadequacies, underscore the risk involved in relying on defaults provided by platform providers. Such contractual uncertainty vastly increases a developer's potential liability, especially concerning apps dealing with sensitive data. Yet, even in instances where there is ostensibly sufficient coverage, a developer should use a EULA specifically tailored to their app and business model. Doing so provides greatly enhanced liability protection and secures yet another variable under a developer's direct supervision and control.

SUMMARY

A developer's first line of defense is its written contracts, protecting everything within the "house" of the company. From founder relationships and employees to incoming and outgoing intellectual property, written agreements are the best way to avoid disputes by obviating them before they arise. A clear, well-written contract defines expectations, sets boundaries and alerts all parties to requirements of performance and penalties.

A written agreement requires several elements in order to be valid. The foremost of those is consideration, a bargained for exchange in which each party receives something of value from the other that induces them to enter into the contract. Without consideration, contracts can be attacked as invalid or completely void. Therefore, it is extremely important to ensure that good, valuable and adequate consideration is factored into every written agreement, even those involving employees and confidentiality.

Contracts involving contractors and employees are especially important, as they define and govern the relationships between a developer and the "crew" that builds the products and carries out ongoing operations. Every employee, including company officers such as the CEO, should have a written and executed employment agreement that specifically lists their position and duties. Likewise, any non-employee contractor should be attached to the company with a written agreement that fully and adequately describes the work they are to perform and the timeframe in which it is done.

In addition to specifying such details, employee and contractor agreements should specify with great particularity the ownership of intellectual property created during the employment or contractual engagement. If the worker is an employee, the contract should clarify that anything created within the scope of that employment is property of the employing company. Likewise, anything generated by an independent contractor should conveyed and assigned to the contracting company.

Similarly, both employees and contractors should be locked into confidentiality and non-disclosure provisions to protect a developer's intellectual property, trade secrets and confidential information. Drafted correctly, these types of provisions can be powerful tools in the event of misappropriation or disclosure of information to third parties. Perhaps even more important than confidentiality is the inclusion of a non-solicitation provision for employees to ensure that a former employee does not recruit other employees away from the company and drain valuable resources from a developer's development team.

Warranties and indemnification are also important elements of contracts and agreements into which a developer enters. These provisions explicitly state what the developer pledges a product will or will not do, and expressly disclaims any warranties that are unnecessarily burdensome or impractical. Additionally, indemnification creates a promise of reimbursement of damages and claims, such as those relating to third-party intellectual property infringement. Indemnification is an excellent resource for putting a contracting party on alert that any resulting harm from use of their product or services must be reimbursed. Doing so lessens the likelihood of a party knowingly using infringing materials or acting in an unauthorized manner.

Arbitration and mediation can literally save a developers hundreds of thousands of dollars and countless hours of time by avoiding litigation. These provisions bind each party to settle disputes using a neutral third-party, whose decision is usually binding, without the necessity or expense of filing a lawsuit. In these proceedings, formal court proceedings are completely avoided to save both parties significant time and expense in settling disputes that could otherwise be potentially devastating.

Licensing can play a significant role for developers, both in content acquisition and resource allocation. Potentially useful software or other elements (graphical, musical or audiovisual) can be licensed for use in a developer's app rather than being produced in-house. This method of acquiring content can prove much more economical than self-developing and thereby reduces expenses and frees resources to be used elsewhere. Likewise, outbound licensing of a developer's content or software can provide a lucrative secondary revenue stream.

The end-user license agreement, a specific outbound license that governs the relationship between a developer and their users should be given special attention. As the main point of legal contact between the creator of software and a user, the EULA is a very important document that determines many of the rights and remedies of both parties.

A developer should always ensure that a customized EULA, tailored specifically for their app, as well as any accompanying web or backend service, is drafted and presented to the user. The default agreements provided by the platform providers are insufficient to cover most developers, especially those producing apps that deal with a user's personal or location-based information or that generate content for submission to third-party or post-processing services.

LAWSUITS

THE DEVIL'S PITCHFORK

The word "litigation" could easily be replaced with "extortion" in most cases, especially those involving intellectual property in the App Era. Developers are terrified of becoming mired in the process, and with good reason. According to the PwC's 2017 Patent Litigation Study, the annual median damages award from was approximately $10.2 million. Even more concerning is that the number of patent infringement lawsuits originating with non-practicing entities, commonly referred to as "patent trolls," continues to rise. Indeed, developers have a great deal to fear in an industry where litigation has become a business model.

A complete analysis of patent trolls and the insufferable corruption and carnage in the patent system is beyond the scope of this book. However, a coder should familiarize themselves with the existence of the issue and learn how to best avoid putting their companies and products directly in the line of fire. This type of strategic analysis is essential to a developer's survival in the App Era. As we have discussed, code and law operate as a unified expression of engineering and intellect. a developer's journey begins with knowing their own vessel, how it functions, its strongest assets and, most importantly, the weak points at which opponents will strike.

Litigation, therefore, is something best prepared for before it happens. It is one thing to expect an attack and plan for its defense in the solemnity of peace and quite another to mount a response as the barbarians storm the gates. Concerning litigation and trolls, there is simply no substitute for a thorough examination of a company's intellectual property portfolio to determine what exists and whether it could potentially be infringing. Obviously, this entails a tremendous amount of work that may seem unjustifiable during the early phases of a developer, during which business manuals recommend focusing primarily on coding.

Yet again, law is something that should not be avoided in such instances for financial or resource reasons. Development time is certainly critical but developers should consider the materials with which they build their houses, as well as the timeline and financial outcome. Further, an intellectual property audit does not necessarily require lengthy or expensive processes. Simply being aware and asking questions can often be enough to root out a developer's issues and avoid future problems. This leads us to the most important lesson to take away from this book—the law's effect on an app and its operation sets and defines a coder's expectations.

Incidentally, the more realistic a developer's expectations, the more they become aware that litigation is less about what has happened than what will happen. For example, many developers react to a pre-litigation demand letter with a sense of shock and bewilderment about what they have done wrong. What they should be spending mental processing time on is tempering their reaction to the likely outcome. If a developer is the unlucky blip on a troll's radar, there is likely some manner of nexus with the claimed patent. Evaluating that connection and determining the risk of litigation versus the impact of settlement and/or feature alteration allows a developer to respond according to the likely outcome.

THE ART OF KNOWING WHAT'S REAL

Patent litigation is but one of many type of lawsuits and disputes in which developers may find themselves embroiled. There are countless causes of action asserted against developers from any different litigants, including employee claims, third-party intellectual property infringement claims, copyright and trademark infringement, breach of contract, negligence, misappropriation and many others. As we have discussed, the core of a developer's defense to these threats is their contracts. As guardians of the gates, a developer's contracts will largely determine the type and scope of claims that are asserted against them.

Still, there are a number of common disputes

faced by developers in the App Era. The most frequent and disruptive are disputes among partners or founders. These types of disputes can usually be anticipated since they are normally precipitated by vocal disagreements, most likely involving money or ownership rights. Foreshadowing is a good thing in these instances because it allows a rational, logical discussion of what can be done to resolve the conflict before litigation. If a developer's business structure and intellectual property foundation have been secured, it is far less likely that such disputes will leave a ruined relationship or catastrophic financial event in its wake.

Less expected, but not altogether surprising, are claims made by former employees or contractors. These disputes can be particularly galling, especially when they come from individuals with whom a developer has had an employment relationship. Typically, true employment opportunities with a developer are rare because of extreme financial pressure. If an employment contract is extended, it is certainly the exception and not the norm. Learning that a former employee, someone who was given a relatively valuable chance at being a part of the company can therefore generate a great deal of disappointment and resentment.

Employee claims tend to revolve around breach of contract or unlawful termination. In other words, someone gets fired and does not agree with the assessment of their performance or the decision to conclude the employment relationship. Former employees may also have claims for negligence, injuries, unpaid compensation or harassment. These claims, unless specifically addressed in the employment agreement, accompanying policies and standards of conduct have the potential to undermine financial stability, rhythm and, worst of all, a developer's relationships with and trust of other employees.

If, however, a developer has taken the time to generate standardized employment agreements, policies and standards for employees, such claims are relatively short lived. a developer should look at employment agreements as a perfect example of contracting around disputes before they begin. Likewise, well-developed policies and standards of performance and conduct provide an employee with clearly defined expectations and succinctly inform them of the role they play. Again, these are relatively inexpensive and simple implementations of legal ideas that can effectively determine either smooth and productive business operations or ongoing and tumultuous conflict.

No matter the dispute, the point of entry for a developer should be to determine whether the matter has already continued to litigation. If there has been service of process (see below), a formal lawsuit has been filed and the diligence level must be elevated accordingly. If, on the other hand, litigation has not yet begun, there is an opportunity to resolve things before they get out of control. While the manner of handling such discussions should be specifically tailored to the situation, a developer should always approach an informal dispute as an opportunity to avoid litigation. Unless there are absolutely no questions regarding the nature or facts of the dispute, the risk of litigation should be the single biggest encouragement to seek an amicable solution.

This is not to say that every dispute that has not entered litigation must be settled. There will certainly be conflicts where the developer is attacked unjustly or without provocation. In those instances, there should be a firm yet tactful presentation of position and an acceptance that should litigation begin, at least the facts are there to support that position. If, on the other hand, a developer can simply not afford the time and expense of litigation, the costs of settlement may outweigh the perception that the dispute is somehow lost. In the App Era, disputes and conflict are less about being right than they are about who survives. After all, if a developer wins a battle but not the war, where does that leave their product and their company?

Winning the war means realizing that many informal disputes that appear to be destined for litigation can be resolved through comparatively simple devices like informal negotiation, arbitration or mediation. Recall that such clauses can be included in contractual agreements that will bind both parties to the decision of a third-party arbitrator. By ensuring that all relevant employee and contractor relationships are subject to such provisions, it is much less likely that litigation will result. Most attorneys are aware of the powerful wedge litigation holds against a defendant and, when that weapon is taken away, the value of the case drops significantly. Potential plaintiffs may therefore decide that their claims are simply not worth pursuing.

LAWYERS, GUNS & MONEY

Many people believe that a lawsuit is about promoting truth, justice, equity or fairness. In reality, once a dispute enters the legal system as litigation, rationality takes a back seat to procedure, posturing and presentation. Lawsuits are the single most uncomfortable and frustrating experience most people will ever experience, apart from perhaps the pain of childbirth, a privilege granted to only half the human population. Litigation stands alone, however, in its capacity for delivering raw, unbridled wretchedness to the broadest audience.

In the United States, the sickness (and greed) of litigation has reached epidemic levels. Lawsuits are launched with little thought and even less planning. The most ridiculous and banal of disputes is likely to wind up mired in the serpentine maze of the court system, presided over by judges whose appearance would be more appropriate in the apocalyptic throng of a zombie apocalypse. The average judge's grasp of technology peaks at the switchover from the rotary-dial to push-button phone. This is, obviously, a bewildering and exhausting state of affairs, especially for developers to whom litigation is as disorienting as the opening lines of Zork, the classic Infocom text adventure:

You are in an open field west of a big white house with a boarded front door. There is a small mailbox here.

The mailbox is opened to reveal a notice of lawsuit and the player is left to stumble about trying to discover how and why things have fallen apart.

Unlike in Zork, however, there is no escape once the floodgates have opened. Although developers will certainly not become litigation experts by the end of this chapter, it is valuable to understand the general framework of a lawsuit, how it works and, most importantly, what to expect.

We will therefore look at the overall structure of a lawsuit by examining its basic process. Again, this discussion is not a substitute for legal advice, especially in the event an actual lawsuit has been filed. It is intended to give developers a survey of the general procedure of a dispute once it has attained sufficient critical mass to be thrust into the formal legal system. Every case and its components are different, so this guide is not meant to be an exhaustive statement possibilities. In an actual lawsuit, it is possible (and very probable) that there would be additional matters to which a litigant would need to address significant attention. However, the following summary of the litigation process should give developers the ability to gain their bearings and establish a foothold in the process from a business perspective.

Before we begin, it is important to note that litigation can be avoided in some instances by the simple addition of an arbitration or mediation clause in a developer's contractual agreements. These provisions legally bind both parties to attempt to settle disputes through an informal process involving a third-party arbitrator or mediator. When averrable, this process is extremely helpful and can result in a settlement agreement that saves both parties significant time and expense. Again, however, the arbitration or mediation clause must be included in a written contract regarding the situation from which the claim arises so it is imperative for a developer to include the provision in all of their written agreements.

THE COMPLAINT

Litigation officially begins with the filing of a "complaint" by the plaintiff, the person who is suing someone. Sometimes referred to as the "petition," this initial filing will list all the various claims, or "causes of action," that the plaintiff believes it can assert against the defendant, the person being sued. The complaint also addresses general procedural issues, such as those relating to the court's jurisdiction over the dispute (the court's authority to even deal with the case) and other matters. Generally, the plaintiff must assert all the claims it has against the defendant in this first document, although it can revise its complaint concerning the causes of action that are listed.

Complaints vary from one type of a lawsuit and court to another, but they share similar form.

Essentially, complaints are an official communication to a court recessing assistance with a particular dispute. As such, complaints will contain some manner of request for a particular type of legal relief, either damages (a "legal" remedy), an injunction or order to do something specific (an "equitable" remedy) or both. If a developer receives a complaint, this is the first section that should draw their attention, as it is crucial to know what the Plaintiff is asking the court to do.

THE ANSWER

After receiving the complaint by "service of process," a formal delivery of the complaint by government officials or a private process server, the defendant will file an answer within a specified timeframe. Filing an answer can be very specific (as usually happens in federal suits where each allegation must be admitted or denied), or the defendant may file a simple general denial requiring that the plaintiff prove every claim included in their complaint. The filing of the answer is within the specified time is extremely important because an unanswered complaint is considered a tacit acceptance of each of the plaintiff's allegations.

Absent an answer, the plaintiff will ask for, and usually receive, a default judgment which essentially states that the plaintiff wins as a result of the defendant not filing an answer. Thus, properly preparing and filing an answer to a complaint is of utmost importance and should be considered the highest priority at the onset of litigation. Of course, if a developer promptly notifies their attorney, the answer will be filed on time and in the proper form. If the situation demands filing of a "pro se" (non-attorney) answer, a developer should definitely take care to find the proper form and respond within the deadline set when they received the complaint. In the event a pro se response is necessary, an attorney should be retained immediately afterwards so that deficiencies in the answer may be corrected and the lawsuit handled properly in future stages.

DISCOVERY

Imagine an adversary gets to bury their opponent up to their neck in sand and kick them in the head while asking questions. This is a fairly accurate description of discovery, the stage of litigation where each side is able to ask questions and request documents from each other. In essence, anything that an opponent has in their possession (albeit with some exceptions like attorney communications) is fair game and must be produced to allow discovery of evidence. There is no easy way around or through the discovery process and it is easily the most frustrating, time consuming element of a lawsuit. Most participants in discovery feel completely exhausted after complying with a seemingly unending series of document requests and interrogatories (written questions).

Responses to interrogatories are critical to the discovery stage, since they usually help an opponent prepare for depositions, interviews in which each party in a dispute may orally question the other. These intensive sessions last for a cumulative period determined by the amount of the claim or general scope of the dispute. It is not uncommon for a deposition to last an entire day, sometimes spanning multiple day-long sessions over several days.

The question and answer process is similar to old-school police interrogations seen on late-night television, but is usually unaccompanied by punches being thrown. Nevertheless, the coffee served at some of them has, on occasion, risen to the level of physical abuse. There is simply no effective method to survive a deposition without the legal knowledge and experience of an attorney who will object to certain questions for various reasons. Therefore, a developer should consider the discovery phase the point at which attorney involvement is mandatory.

MOTIONS -OR- WHERE THE MONEY GOES

Following discovery but before trial begins, each side will be able to make various motions, such as requests to exclude certain evidence obtained in discovery. If the evidence obtained in discovery overwhelmingly supports or disproves a particular claim, the respective party may move for summary judgment to effectively dismiss the case and end the lawsuit. These types of motions are complex and require a significant investment of time and careful analysis of the evidence obtained in discovery. Again, no developer should be at the pre-trial phase without legal representation.

It is important to note that most settlements are reached at this point, after properly gauging the evidence in the opponent's possession. Likewise, some lawsuits may be referred to arbitration or mediation, depending on the circumstances. Whatever the case, if a settlement is reached, it is likely to be the result of whatever is discovered during the discovery phase and a direct result of assessing the risk involved in moving forward with the lawsuit. The more damaging the discovery obtained, the higher probability of paying a larger settlement and vice-versa. The settlement amount notwithstanding, it will become increasingly clear at this point whether going forward to trial is a viable option given the risk.

TRIAL

In the unfortunate even that a lawsuit is not settled during or after the discovery period, the matter will continue to trial. At this point, both parties will usually attempt to reach a settlement or some manner of compromise. This dealmaking process is prompted by attorneys, who are well acquainted with a trial's propensity to eat through money and have a tendency to deliver shockingly unexpected results. A well-balanced settlement is therefore supported by most lawyers, perhaps even more so by those specializing in the vagaries and inconsistencies of trial work.

In addition to being jaw droopingly expensive, a trial is the ultimate sinkhole of time and energy. Entire months can be shaved off the lives of previously mirthful people who would otherwise be contributing something of value to the world, with the obvious exception of trolls. But this is where plaintiffs, and particularly non-practicing entities that fancy themselves innovators, excel. Often, a troll will have significant resources at their disposal to mount and manage a trial, whereas most solo and indie developers cannot. The result is a veritable misery machine that sucks lifeblood from a developer as hungrily as brooding vampires in teen sexploitation dramas. There is no mechanism known to man capable of exacting its toll in a more efficient, and often blindingly spectacular fashion, than an adversarial trial.

Opposed to what is seen in movies and television shows, trials are not at all sexy, interesting or dramatic. There are some relatively engaging, intense moments during examination of witnesses but if a developer is looking for excitement or drama, they should tune into the latest edition of CSI. That said, there is one moment in trial when at least the majority of people in the room are paying attention, especially the litigants, and that is the delivery of the verdict (assuming a jury trial). Yet even the verdict is not incontrovertible, as anyone who follows the ever developing romantic-comedy of Apple-Samsung dispute(s) can attest. There are various instances where a judge can set aside a jury verdict and enter a completely different result, often causing a great deal of surprise, shock and further misery to the participants.

APPEAL

Unsurprisingly, the appeal process is designed to allow those litigants who feel they have received the short end of the stick in the trial game to attempt to change the result. Contrary to popular belief, however, an appeal is not a complete "do-over" of a trial and can only be pursued if there are elements of the trial in which the judge or jury made an error. For example, if a judge erroneously allows evidence into the trial for consideration that should not have been admitted because of a clear rule, that point may be argued in the appeal. Even then, an attorney seeking to appeal a decision based on such a point must have objected to the error during the trial to preserve the issue for the resulting appeal.

If this seems like an excessively complex game of

cat and mouse with procedure and rules, it is because the description is fitting. Developers should be sensing by now that the litigation process is not something that can taken lightly or handled indiscriminately. If possible, litigation should be avoided, like a loathsome disease, by careful and systematic observation of their business, products, intellectual assets and operations. Quite simply, developers in the App Era are destined for litigation unless they adequately prepare otherwise. Everything a developer does in their legal and business operation, from inception of an idea through development to the first sale, determines their fate. If litigation is to be avoided, it must be defeated before it begins.

THE BEST DEFENSE

In The Karate Kid Part II, Mr. Miyagi tells Daniel that the best way to block a punch is to not be present when the punch arrives. This is quite possibly the best legal advice ever given, not to mention an effective strategy to avoid broken teeth. Similar to a street fight, a plaintiff in a lawsuit lashes out with a series of attacks on a defendant, often resulting in a Fight Club worthy bare-knuckle brawl that leaves everyone beaten senseless. The best defense, as Miyagi suggests, is to avoid being pulled into it in the first place. It sounds rudimentary and obvious but the best strategy for dealing with adversarial legal proceedings is to simply not be involved in them. If a developer focuses as much on building their "house" as they do their products, the resulting experience will be much less confrontational and litigious.

This results for a variety of reasons but, primarily, the methodology of creating a business structure in the App Era is by looking forward rather than merely within. If a developer focuses all of their time and effort on the product, the vehicle used to sell that product, as well as its core, will be susceptible to challenges. Essentially, it is the classic Fast/Good/Cheap triangular development model but applied to the entire enterprise rather than the product alone. Generally, fast and cheap yields poor quality or, in the context of litigation risk assessment, high potential liability. Just as bugs in code can make things crash, slow down development and ultimately ruin an otherwise good product, litigation should be viewed as a bug that plagues overall business structure, strategy and well-being.

The point developers must reach is tacit acceptance that bugs will exist. It is virtually impossible to code for a complete absence of bugs, mostly because all development work is done in the vacuum of a developer's space. Out in the wild where users flog, beat and pistol whip apps with increasingly bizarre behaviors, software bugs are a naturally occurring phenomenon. Similarly, business bugs (litigation) cannot be planned around. There will always be some risk, no matter how slight, or some incalculable happening that defies all logic and reason. Developers must therefore embrace effective litigation risk management strategies, much like they implement software bug management systems in their development process and methodologies.

Legal risk assessment, tracking and management are therefore as critical to a developer's business as crafting clean code. All of these things depend not so much on a developer's willingness to hire a lawyer as they do simple observation and evaluation of their business structure, intellectual property and contractual relationships. An awareness of the overall threat level in the industry and participation in the cumulative experience of the developer community illuminates looming threats and, similarly, obvious solutions to a developer's litigation risk.

For example, surveying the current legal landscape reveals that trolls based in the United States (as they typically are) are reluctant to fully litigate claims against non-United States entities absent significant amounts of recoverable revenue. This analysis produces very useful data concerning business structuring scenarios, as discussed earlier in the book. It also helps developers evaluate their products and intellectual property against the threat level presented by the markets in which they do business. Ultimately, this can result in a decision to stop offering products in the United States, viewed as a mosh-pit full of pissed-off and angry potential plaintiffs. This highlights the hugely negative effect of the patent war on the app industry and its true victim—the users.

Given the current situation, a developer must arm themselves with a thorough understanding of their apps, potentially harmful patents and a risk assessment of the markets where they wish to do business. Again, most developers will deal with patents in responding to trolls or assessing risk rather than registering their own patents. However, the same degree of analysis and response should govern a developer's intellectual property portfolio. In discerning whether products are protectable, overlap with existing patents or those elements that may be claimed as infringing will be revealed. This yields a realistic threat assessment and alerts developers of possible claims before they occur, allowing them to avoid the punch by simply not being there.

SUMMARY

There are a variety of reasons a lawsuit may be filed and innumerable theories of legal claims and liability. However, litigation really amounts to nothing more than a silly sideshow that draws a developer's attention away from making great apps. Unfortunately, in the App Era, litigation has become a lucrative business model for technology trolls and others that aspire to extort a developer's profits and value. It is a sad and pathetic system that has allowed this model to proposer while developers, the true creators of the app revolution are forced to choose draconian licensing arrangement or financial extermination.

Still, a developer's most frequent disputes will likely come not from trolls but former employees, contractors and contractual relationships. These conflicts are among the most challenging a developer will face because they involve individuals and partners that may have been integral to the company's foundation. Most of these disputes will be focused on financial claims that will be easy to solve if proper business structuring, intellectual property management and contract formation have taken place. Disputes are much easier to resolve if a developer has followed a business path combining code and law into a cohesive strategy.

Sadly, non-litigation disputes and lawsuits are legal facts that must be addressed with an informed, rational approach to solving the problem. Pre-litigation disputes are typically much simpler to resolve and can usually be settled or effectively squashed before achieving critical mass. Once filed as a lawsuit, however, a conflict takes on an entirely new life of its own, devoid of sanity, logic and reason. Lawsuits are an elaborate maze of procedure and posturing best delegated to an attorney. There is simply no reason for a developer to venture into court alone, especially given the potentially crushing judgments that can result from certain types of cases.

However, it is important for a solo or indie developer to familiarize themselves with the basic process of litigation, which begins with the filing of a complaint by the suing party. After filing, the complaint must be officially delivered to the person being sued, who is then given the opportunity to respond and assert whatever defenses may be available. Afterwards, a period of evidence gathering called discovery begins which is a series of written questions and answers followed by oral interviews of witnesses. Following the collection of evidence by both parties, pretrial motions will occur, sometimes with a particular party attempting to end the lawsuit early with a judgment in their favor based on favorable evidence they obtained in discovery.

If the disputes remains unsettled after all the initial filings, discovery and motions are completed, a formal trial will be held, sometimes including a jury. A trial is an extremely complex and risky procedure, mostly because of the introduction of a new set of variables—jurors—into the equation. This is the single most dangerous phase of litigation where even a relatively favorable set of facts can be turned into an unexpected loss. Regardless of outcome, however, there will surely be an appeal following the delivery of the verdict in the trial. Unlike trials, appeals are specialized procedures that follow unique procedural rules.

Because litigation is such an expensive, time consuming and sometimes surprising process, developers should pursue as many litigation avoidance strategies as possible. These include the topics discussed thus far, such as solid business structuring, intellectual property protection and drafting a unique set of contracts that contain risk avoidance provisions. Contractual language limiting liability and disclaiming warranties effectively shunt liability away from a developer's business. Additionally, a provision requiring binding arbitration is one of the simplest and easiest methods to sidestep litigation before it begins.

CLOSING THOUGHTS

CLOSING THOUGHTS

If there is one word in this book that stood out, I hope that word is survival.

The App Era is a heady, exhilarating time that is seemingly filled with endless possibilities. Look past the marketing speak and typical tech industry puffery, however, and you will see a world filled with limitless danger for unprepared developers. Apps have dominated the software industry for the past decade and there is no greater time in history to be a coder. But rushing into this world without an awareness of the legal and business risks is one of the most foolhardy mistakes a developer can make.

There is no way to escape the issues presented here if a developer is releasing their apps into the modern marketplace. Hopefully, the chapters above have given you a broad overview of those issues and ways they define modern coding.

What now?

What should a developer do with the wealth of legal gibberish and buzzwords they have learned? There are many ways to proceed from here, including the hiring of an expensive legal team that would love nothing more than to collect a fat retainer, which will be plowed through in under a month. Whether a developer does the work themselves or hires professional assistance, however, the first step should be sitting down in a quiet room and simply thinking about their business.

I encourage developers to start that process with

the following questions:

1. How do I structure my business to minimize legal risks and adequately protect my assets and those of the company I am trying to create?

2. What are my core intellectual properties and how do I adequately protect them while simultaneously leveraging their value?

3. Have I implemented written contracts for the business and intellectual property elements of my business and do those contracts adequately protect the business from legal risk?

4. Have I structured my business and intellectual assets in such a way (through contracts and other means) to effectively reduce the risk of being sued and, if I am sued anyway, do those structures provide defenses and strategies to help with the

litigation?

While answering these questions, coders should refer to the appropriate sections in this book. Once the answers begin to appear, it is hoped that developers will begin to view their businesses in a more legal focused way. To assist in the process, follow the "What Now?" Worksheet that follows.

I hope this book has been beneficial to all that have read it. I wish your company and apps the best of luck and a successful future!

THE TAKEAWAY

✓ Choose a legal entity structure that is best for your business situation.

- If you are a one-owner company, look into LLCs or other hybrid entities. They offer the best combination of asset protection and flexibility. There are reduced documentation requirements and, in most jurisdictions, are relatively inexpensive to set up and keep running.

- If you are a two-owner development company, an LLC may also be a good choice, especially with its minimal documentation requirements. If your development partner is a sophisticated investor, check with a financial professional on whether a limited partnership would be a good option for you. If you select a partnership and are selected to be the general partner, ensure that you form a personal LLC or corporation to specifically name as the general partners to avoid personal liability.

- If your development company is composed of multiple owners and the goal is to attract venture financing for later growth, a corporation is a solid choice. Investors are more familiar with the corporate form compared to LLCs and partnerships and will likely require a corporate formation. Selection of the corporate form may save some time later in the investment process. Note, however, that the documentation and meeting requirement are significantly more burdensome than the other forms, so having at least one shareholder that is familiar with record keeping would be ideal in this instance.

- Always comply with any statute specific reporting or disclosure requirements. Failure to do so could result in dissolution of the legal entity and eliminate all of the asset protection you have worked to achieve.

✓ Review and analyze your company's intellectual property and formulate a plan to leverage each asset in the best possible way.

- The copyright to all written, pictorial, graphic, audio and visual works should be formally registered as early as possible. Doing so ensures that you will have access to statutory damages in the event of infringement.

- Any marks, logos or brand names that your company is using or intends to use should be formally registered as soon as possible after the first use (or an "intent to use" declaration filed). This ensures that your valuable logos and branding are protected and increase in value.

- Ensure that any intellectual property not created in-house is properly licensed for the use (and scope of use, i.e. commercial sales) for which they are intended. This can include stock photos and artwork purchased from stock agencies. Check each license to ensure that your use does not exceed the scope of the license.

- Carefully review your apps for processes that would rise to the level of being granted a software patent. This is an extremely complex endeavor and requires a great deal of time and effort. Generally, you should be seeking this level of protection for truly unique and "groundbreaking" processes.

- Carefully monitor your company's secret processes, formulas, customer lists and other "non-statutory" intellectual properties. In certain instances, some intellectual assets may be best protected as a trade secret rather than disclosed in a patent application.

✓ Maintain written, dated and executed contracts for each transaction or contemplated transaction a and with each consultant, contractor, employee and vendor with whom your company engages.

- Ensure that all contracts with

consultants, employees and vendor properly recite the company's ownership of its intellectual properties and provide for penalties in the event those properties are used without permission.

- Include a solid non-disclosure and confidentiality agreement in all consultant and employee contracts.

- Include warrantees and indemnification provisions in each contract to avoid conflicts over the other party's duties in the transaction.

- Include arbitration and/or mediation provisions in each contract so that you have an informal dispute resolution process to lean on prior to starting any formal lawsuit. These methods can save hundreds of thousands of dollars in hotly contested matters.

- Maintain proper license agreements for each intellectual asset that comes into and goes out of the company. In other words, if you are using a third-party asset in your app, have a license for its use. Likewise, if you are allowing a third-party to use a company asset, have a license in place that recites the company's compensation for such use.

✓ Put in the time, do the work and avoid the pain and suffering of a lawsuit.

- If you receive a pre-litigation

demand, i.e. a threatening letter that arrives before a lawsuit is started, consult with an attorney to best judge the legal threat.

- If you have properly structured your business and its operations, the greatest threats will be from patent trolls. If you receive a demand from a troll, work with a qualified professional to assess the level of the threat to your business and the option of settlement.

- If you are sued, you must hire a qualified professional to handle your specific matter. It will cost a great deal of money and be more intimidating and painful than the worst dentist visit you have ever had. Hunker down, find points for argument and weather the storm. You and your company will survive if you remain steadfast.